MUSEUM

THE STORY OF AMERICA'S TREASURE HOUSES

by *Alvin Schwartz*

Illustrated with photographs
E. P. Dutton & Co., Inc. NEW YORK

The following sources for chapter opening photographs are gratefully acknowledged: page 17, Los Angeles County Museum of Natural History; page 47, Art Institute of Chicago; page 123, Milwaukee Public Museum; page 174, Field Museum of Natural History; page 222, Franklin Institute, photograph by Herbert K. Barnett.

How the Information for
This Book Was Gathered

IN SETTING OUT TO WRITE A BOOK ABOUT MUSEUMS, I QUICKLY DIS-
covered that they are complicated places in the midst of great
change. I also soon found that most have their own ways of doing
things. As a result, I spent months interviewing staff members at
museums of all kinds and sizes throughout the United States. In
the end, lengthy interviews had been conducted at forty-six
museums in fifteen states and the District of Columbia. I also
visited another three dozen museums just to study the exhibits. In
addition, I corresponded and talked by telephone with persons
at scores of other museums.

Along with learning a good deal about museums themselves, I
also learned a fair amount about museum people. I can say with
all sincerity that it would be difficult to find a more generous and
more interesting group in any profession. For the time they
devoted to my questions and for the information and insights they
provided, I am sincerely grateful. The listing below includes those
persons I interviewed and those who helped me in other ways at
museums and related organizations I visited.

BINGHAMTON, NEW YORK: Roberson Memorial Center, Keith
Martin.

BLOOMFIELD HILLS, MICHIGAN: Cranbrook Institute of Science,
Robert T. Hatt, Charles Gosser, Mrs. Donald Odle.

BOSTON: Museum of Fine Arts, Dows Dunham, William J. Young,
Diggory Venn, Susan Wilson; Museum of Science, Caroline Harri-
son, Chan Waldrin, James F. Moore; The Children's Museum,
Michael Spock.

CHARLESTON, SOUTH CAROLINA: The Charlestown Museum,
E. Milby Burton.

CHICAGO: Art Institute of Chicago, Charles C. Cunningham, Bar-
bara Wriston, Marcia Fergestad, Martha Bennett King, Thelma
Heagstedt, Barbara Sedelmaier; Chicago Historical Society,
Clement M. Silvestro, Jr., Sarajane Wells, Beatrix Rumford; Field

Museum of Natural History, E. Leland Webber, Loren Woods, Phil Clark; Chicago Museum of Science and Industry, D. M. MacMaster.

COOPERSTOWN, NEW YORK: New York State Historical Association museums, Fred L. Rath, Jr., Minor Wine Thomas.

CORNING, NEW YORK: Corning Museum of Glass, Kenneth Wilson.

DAYTON, OHIO: Dayton Museum of Natural History, E. J. Koestner, Tom Huels; Air Force Museum, Richard E. Baughman.

DETROIT: Detroit Historical Museum, Henry D. Brown, Bartlett M. Frost, Daniel Kinsler; Dossin Great Lakes Museum, Robert E. Lee.

DISTRICT OF COLUMBIA: United States National Museum, Frank A. Taylor, John E. Anglim; Museum of History and Technology, Mendel L. Peterson; Museum of Natural History, Richard B. Woodbury; National Gallery of Art, J. Carter Brown, Margaret I. Bouton, Grose Evans, Peter Davidock, William W. Morrison; National Park Service Museums, Ralph Lewis; The National Historical Wax Museum, Frank L. Dennis, James S. Burris; American Association of Museums, Carolyn H. Wells, Betty Lee Barnes.

LOS ANGELES: California Museum of Science and Industry, H. R. Hopps, Jr., Walter Voll, Joseph M. Head, William C. O'Donnell; Los Angeles County Museum of Natural History, Herbert Friedmann, Charles L. Hogue, Donovan Roberts.

MILWAUKEE: Milwaukee Public Museum, Stephan Borhegyi, Ellen McComb.

MINNEAPOLIS: Minneapolis Institute of Arts, Samuel Sachs II, G. H. Dorr III.

MOUNT VERNON, VIRGINIA: Mount Vernon, Charles C. Wall.

NEW YORK: Metropolitan Museum of Art, Randolph Bullock, Helmut Nickel, Nora E. Scott, Kate C. Lefferts, Thomas Folds, Louise Condit, Constantine Raitzsky, Eleanor Falcon, Katherine Warwick; American Museum of Natural History, Bobb Schaeffer, Gordon Reekie, George Peterson, David J. Schwendeman; Museum of Modern Art, Elizabeth Shaw, Paul J. Harris, Dorthy H. Dudley; Museum of the City of New York, Ralph R. Miller, Albert K. Baragwanath, Helen K. Thomas.

PHILADELPHIA: Philadelphia Museum of Art, Hobart L. Williams, Kneeland McNulty, Frank P. Graham; Independence National

Historical Park, David Wallace; Franklin Institute, Robert L. Neathery, I. M. Levitt, Dean B. Ivey, E. H. Nelson, W. R. Wolf; University Museum, David Crownover.

PORTLAND, OREGON: Oregon Historical Society, Harry Lichter, Robert C. Scott; Portland Art Museum, Francis J. Newton, Rachael Griffin; Oregon Museum of Science and Industry, Clint Gruber.

PRINCETON, NEW JERSEY: Princeton Junior Museum, Mildred Goldberger.

SAINT PAUL, MINNESOTA: The Science Museum, Philip S. Taylor, Bruce R. Erickson; Minnesota Historical Society, Margaret Kimball, Chester Kozlak.

SAN FRANCISCO: California Academy of Sciences, George E. Lindsay; M. H. De Young Memorial Museum, Roger Broussal, Charles Long; San Francisco Maritime Museum, Harlan Soeten.

SEATTLE: Seattle Art Museum, Richard B. Fuller, Edward B. Thomas, Betty Bowen; Pacific Science Center, Robert L. Smallman; Seattle Museum of History and Industry, Mrs. Elizabeth Sutton Gustison, Robert Lussier, Minnie Hanson.

TRENTON, NEW JERSEY: New Jersey State Museum, Kenneth W. Prescott, Patricia Marchiando, Pearl Seligman, Kathryn Greywacz.

The following organizations and individuals also were of great help:

The American Federation of Arts, Robert H. Luck; American Association for State and Local History, William T. Alderson; Brooklyn Museum, Jean L. Keith; Carnegie Corporation; City Art Museum of St. Louis, Thelma Stockho; The Cleveland Museum of Art, Constance Gill; Colonial Williamsburg, Hugh DeSamper; Cranbrook Art Gallery, Bloomfield Hills, Michigan; Isaac Delgado Museum of Art, New Orleans, James B. Byrnes; Detroit Institute of Arts, Robert E. Springer, Robert R. Rodgers; The Ford Foundation, Marcia T. Thompson, Harold A. Klein; Hagley Museum, Wilmington, Delaware, Joseph P. Monigle; Hinsdale Health Museum, Hinsdale, Illinois; Honeywell, Inc.; Jarrell-Ash Company, Frederick Brech; The Jewish Museum, Mimi Shorr; *Mademoiselle;* Mystic Seaport, Alma Eshenfelder;

National Science Foundation, Robert D. Paine, Jr.; National Trust for Historic Preservation, Glenn E. Thompson; William Rockhill Nelson Gallery of Art, Kansas City, Missouri, James E. Seidelman; Newark Museum, Newark, New Jersey; The Norwegian-American Museum, Decorah, Iowa, Betty Seegmiller; Old Sturbridge Village, Sturbridge, Massachusetts, John E. Auchmoody; The Rockefeller Foundation, Elizabeth A. Widenmann; The Society for the Preservation of New England Antiquities, E. Florence Addison; The Smithsonian Institution, B. Richard Berg; Stone Mountain Park, Stone Mountain, Georgia; Dorothy M. Swaringen; The Toledo Museum of Art, Toledo, Ohio, Charles F. Gunther; Virginia Museum of Fine Arts, Richmond, Virginia, Fred Haseltine, Mrs. Alma Walton; The Henry Francis du Pont Winterthur Museum, Winterthur, Delaware, Dorothy W. Greer; State Historical Society of Wisconsin, John W. Winn.

Books, museum journals, magazines, reports, and newspapers were still other sources of information. The books I turned to included *The Proud Possessors* by Aline Saarinen (New York: Random House, 1958), *Museums U.S.A.: A History and Guide* by Herbert and Marjorie Katz (New York: Doubleday & Co., 1965), *The Smithsonian Institution* by Walter Karp (New York: *American Heritage* magazine, 1965), *National Gallery of Art, Washington, D.C.* by John Walker (New York: Harry N. Abrams, Inc.), *The Tastemakers* by Russell Lynes (New York: Harper, 1954), *The Egyptian Department and Its Excavations* by Dows Dunham (Boston: Museum of Fine Arts, 1958), and *Museum Directory of the United States and Canada* (American Association of Museums, 1966).

Museum journals of particular help were *Museum News* published by the American Association of Museums, *Curator* published by the American Museum of Natural History, and *Proceedings of the California Academy of Sciences*.

The magazine article "Behind New York's Window on Nature" in the February, 1963, *National Geographic* provided valuable supplementary information about the American Museum of

Natural History. Annual reports of various museums were a fascinating source of information on museum finances, activities, and philosophy. Accounts in the New York *Times* of developments in the museum field also were extremely useful.

Finally, I am deeply grateful to my wife, Barbara Carmer Schwartz, for the countless contributions she made as preparation of this book progressed.

ALVIN SCHWARTZ

Contents

MUSEUM

THE ARKANSAS ARTS CENTER
MacArthur Park
Little Rock, Arkansas

1 | Years of Change

IT MAY SEEM FAR-FETCHED TO COMPARE THE ART INSTITUTE OF Chicago or the California Academy of Sciences in San Francisco or any other museum with Cinderella, but there are similarities. In the years before World War II, most museums were unattractive, wearisome places, often no more interesting to a visitor than a well-kept storeroom. Many were run by the wealthy and socially prominent largely in line with their own interests and those of scholars. But even publicly owned museums were uninspired, gloomy places which left one not with a thirst for knowledge but with glazed eyes and tired feet. Although many such museums were important institutions, the public was not enthusiastic about them. Nor, it must be admitted, were many museums enthusiastic about the public.

In the 1950's things began to change, not only for museums, but also for the theatre, the symphony orchestras, the ballet, and other such organizations as the public, in greatly increased numbers, began turning to the pleasures of culture and knowledge.

There were several reasons for this "cultural explosion," as it came to be known. With a shorter work week, people had more time for leisure than in the past. With higher pay, they had more money to spend. Through travel and TV, they got to see more. With more education, they read more. The result was that people in general in the mid-twentieth century knew more about their world and had broader interests than had previous generations.

Museums were affected in a number of ways. Attendance began to climb, and museums began to place far more emphasis than in the past on the public's interests and needs. In addition, the number of museums began to increase, particularly in smaller communities.

Today change continues. As this is written there are some five thousand museums in the United States, over a thousand more than there were in 1950. New museums open at the remarkable rate of one every three and a half days. Attendance also rises steadily; in a recent year there were over 300 million visits.[1]

In their efforts to serve the public better and attract a still larger attendance, many museums have changed in dramatic fashion. They have improved their exhibits by displaying less and by showing it more attractively. In a growing number of history and science museums, specimens are now used to illustrate a story or explain a concept rather than for their own sakes as in the past. Color, sound, animation, and other modern exhibiting techniques

---

[1] Some examples: Metropolitan Museum of Art, New York, 6,281,162; Smithsonian Museum of Natural History, Washington, D.C., 3,051,472; Art Institute of Chicago, 1,792,103; Henry Ford Museum and Greenfield Village, Dearborn, Michigan, 1,401,394; George Washington's home at Mount Vernon, Virginia, 1,309,000; Detroit Museum of Arts, 674,635; Plimoth Plantation, Plymouth, Massachusetts, 480,000; Museum of Science, Boston, 463,353; Kansas City Museum of History and Science, 112,393.

also are being put to work. Museums have made their galleries easier to visit through the use of tours, lectures, demonstrations, "talking labels," guidebooks, and portable tape-recorded guides. They have also vastly expanded their services to schools, not only with tours and classes, but in some cases through the use of art, science, and history-mobiles that travel to classrooms hundreds of miles away.

For both adults and children, there are workshops, films, courses, field trips, concerts, dance recitals, puppet shows, plays, even folk festivals. Museums also publish books and magazines, produce TV and radio shows, and operate stores where one can buy all sorts of things that have to do with the museum's field of interest. For the convenience of visitors, they maintain restaurants, cafeterias, coffee shops, and picnic rooms.[2]

Most publicize their exhibits and services with great vigor. To build attendance and change its image from that of a place run primarily for the well-to-do, the once-staid Museum of Fine Arts in Boston took ads on the backs of taxicabs, reminding Bostonians that the museum was *theirs* to use. To gain nationwide attention, the once equally staid Philadelphia Museum of Art served as a handsome setting for a TV show which featured the singer Barbra Streisand performing amid priceless sculptures and paintings.

Using a revolutionary approach for their field, museums are also beginning to reach out to adults and children in poorer sections by means of small neighborhood museums. The Smithsonian Institution plans to open a storefront "drop in" museum in the Anacostia section of Washington. The Whitney Museum of American Art is planning a neighborhood museum in one of New York City's poorer areas. In addition, the Brooklyn Museum is considering the possibility of hanging art works in laundromats, where people usually have lots of time to think and look.

[2] But the millionth visitor to the National Gallery of Canada explained sheepishly that he really had not come to see the museum's art works, but only to eat in its cafeteria.

To many on museum staffs the surge in attendance has been a source of considerable satisfaction. Lloyd Goodrich, director of the Whitney Museum, told an interviewer, "One of the extraordinary things in my thirty-five years in museum work has been to see the audience increasing not only in numbers but in intelligence." Others see greater attendance as a source of greater support and a chance at long last for greater expansion of their programs. But not everyone feels this way. Some are fearful that the Law of Raspberry Jam is at work. The wider culture is spread, they warn, the thinner, the less meaningful it becomes. One critic believes that the audience for museums has changed from "a small body of connoisseurs to a large body of ignoramuses." A curator of paintings in a West Coast museum called the rise in museum attendance "fantastic and unfortunate. . . . People are not looking," he said. "Even trained observers could get nothing from a gallery at the speed with which today's visitors move through. . . . Museums are not carnivals. They are for serious-minded people." Still other observers are concerned that the emphasis on activities for the public is causing museums—which are chronically short of money and staff—to neglect their responsibilities to research and scholarship.

One of the traditional roles of the museum is that of treasure house and research center. In the art museum the emphasis is on collecting the very finest original examples of man's creativity over thousands of years of civilization. In the history museum the commonplace is sought as well as the rare and valuable, since both are needed to illustrate the story of man's experience. In the natural history museum specimens of nature's variety are collected so that we may better understand the world in which we live. Traditionally the best of a museum's collections are displayed and explained. The collections are also intensively studied by the museum staff, and where they yield new knowledge this is shared with other scholars. Beyond this, the collections are cared for and preserved as part of man's heritage. Together they comprise a

A 12th century Madonna rescued from obscurity and decay, now preserved, studied, and displayed at Boston's Museum of Fine Arts. *Courtesy Museum of Fine Arts, Boston*

library of objects to which others in the future also can turn for knowledge and for pleasure.

A twelfth century Madonna is a case in point. After World War II, representatives of Boston's Museum of Fine Arts found in Paris a neglected, whitewashed wooden figure of the Virgin and Child which they recognized as an art treasure from the Middle Ages. The museum purchased the statue and restored it to its original beauty. However, as Diggory Venn of the museum's staff has written, acquisition "is a beginning, not an end. The Madonna becomes art history, recorded by the Registrar; described, explained, and documented in the Museum *Bulletin;* the subject of gallery talks, lectures, and television programs; copied by art students; photographed and described in books, magazines, learned journals and newspapers; available to the eyes of 750,000 visitors a year; and guarded against the erosions of time. . . ."[3]

The museum's other responsibility is to teach. In recent years education programs for school children and also for adults have become a major activity in almost all museums. In fact, at some museums the listings of tours, classes, lectures, and workshops fill entire catalogs. One reason for this activity is that the need exists to supplement and enrich what the schools offer in the arts, sciences, and history; with their collections and trained staffs, museums often are the logical organizations to do this. Another reason is that government funds frequently are available for such programs. It also is true that education programs build community interest in a museum and encourage greater attendance, which are important objectives of most museums these days.

The growing role of the museum as educator also has seen the development of a new kind of museum, one not concerned with collections, research, or scholarship. Its only interest, in fact, is education. As the men and women who operate these museums see it, their sole functions are to explain, to teach, and to stimulate. In some cases they are concerned only with the fine arts and the performing arts. In others they try to deal with virtually everything. They serve the schools and the public through classes, workshops, demonstrations, performances, and exhibits that often are rented or borrowed from larger institutions. Such museums function as community cultural centers in a growing number of cities and towns throughout the United States. One of the most successful is the Roberson Memorial Center in Binghamton, New York, which serves an eleven-county area in New York and Pennsylvania. Its letterhead reads:

Art   History   Science   Music   Theatre   Dance   Nature
Photography   World Affairs

[3] *Bulletin,* Museum of Fine Arts, Boston; Volume 62, Number 327, 1964.

One soon realizes that it means what it says. The center does have small collections—some birds and minerals, a few historical dioramas, a number of art objects borrowed from the Metropolitan Museum of Art—but its strength lies in the amazing number of classes it offers; in the traveling exhibits it develops and sends to the schools, on subjects ranging from steam power to ancient art; and in its cultural programs. It sponsors a ballet company, a civic theatre, a symphony orchestra, a community opera, and a writers' workshop. For a year it had an artist-in-residence who taught, lectured, and painted, using the center as his base.

The center regularly sends its orchestra or a pianist to perform in rural schools whose pupils otherwise would not have such experiences. When the pianist travels, a van accompanies him with a Steinway grand piano so that he will have a proper instrument to

As part of its broad cultural program, the Roberson Memorial Center in Binghamton, New York, brought these members of a New York City theatre group to its area to perform for high school students. *Courtesy Roberson Memorial Center*

play wherever he appears. Not too long ago, the center arranged for actors and actresses from New York's celebrated Phoenix Theatre group to appear in schools throughout its area. They performed, gave readings, and even conducted workshops for the dramatic clubs.

Science and industry museums, health museums, children's museums, and junior nature centers are other kinds of museums without significant collections whose numbers are steadily increasing. One of the most interesting of these is The Children's Museum in Boston which has turned itself into a kind of laboratory. Its staff has been conducting a set of experiments to determine which types of exhibits teach most effectively. Another experimental program, made possible by Federal funds, involves new uses for museum materials in classrooms. "We are continually exploring the boundaries of what is meant by a museum and by a museum experience," the director, Michael Spock, told me. "At this point, we are not sure that anybody really knows."

NINE MUSES

Some 2,500 years ago there was more certainty. In those days the sister of Belshazzar, ruler of the kingdom of Babylonia, collected ancient objects with a single purpose: to preserve them "for the marvel of beholders." The first important institution to call itself a museum was a university center and library established in 330 B.C. at the Egyptian port city of Alexandria. Yet the description "museum" certainly was accurate if one considers the word's origin. It comes from the Greek *mouseion,* which means a place of inspiration and learning dedicated to the Muses, nine mythological goddesses who ruled over the arts and sciences.[4]

Almost two thousand years were to elapse, however, before

---

[4] The Nine Muses: Calliope, epic poetry and eloquence; Euterpe, music or lyric poetry; Erato, poetry of love; Polymnia, oratory or sacred poetry; Clio, history; Melpomene, tragedy; Thalia, comedy; Terpsichore, choral song and dance; Urania, astronomy.

museums as we know them today began to take shape. Their origins date to the European Renaissance of the fifteenth and sixteenth centuries, that great period of cultural development, scientific discovery, exploration, and commercial growth which served as a bridge between the Middle Ages and modern times. In this period, kings, princes, and other wealthy people began assembling paintings, sculpture, natural history specimens, and curiosities. They displayed their collections in cabinets or cases or at times in galleries they had built onto their homes. The churches also were building collections in this period, but their focus was of course largely religious art. Such collections became the basis of great museums, including the Ashmolean which was established at Oxford University in 1683, the British Museum of London which dates from 1753, and Spain's National Museum which came into being in 1776. However, it was not until the pressures of the French Revolution were felt some years later that most of the collections, including those at the Louvre in Paris, began to be exposed to public view.

The first American museum was established in Charleston, South Carolina, in 1773 with the purpose of "promoting a Natural History" of that area. Four curators were appointed and a newspaper advertisement was run which requested donations from the public. The first acquisition recorded was a drawing of a bird's head. Eleven years later in Philadelphia, the famous portrait artist Charles Willson Peale turned a wing of his home into a public museum. There he displayed portraits he had painted and some natural history specimens. When his collection grew too large for his home, he moved it to the American Philosophical Society's building on 5th near Chestnut and then in 1802 around the corner to Independence Hall, which by that time was vacant. As we shall see later in the section "Natural History Museums," Peale was also the nation's earliest taxidermist of note and very likely its first hunter of dinosaur bones.[5] In addition, he helped establish

---

[5] He also invented a velocipede, a new kind of eyeglasses, and a new type of false teeth.

two other museums: in 1805, the Pennsylvania Academy of the
Fine Arts in Philadelphia, the oldest art museum in the United
States today; in 1814, Peale's Baltimore Museum which was
opened by two of his sons, Rembrandt and Rubens. The Baltimore Museum also is of interest because of its building which was
the first in the United States especially constructed to house a
museum. Although the Baltimore Museum eventually closed, its
building today is home to Baltimore's municipal museum which is
known as the Peale Museum.

The Baltimore Museum and the Pennsylvania Academy of the
Fine Arts in Philadelphia represented two types of American
museums which would develop over the next half century. The
museum in Baltimore was one of the first side-show museums. It
was billed as an "elegant *Rendezvous* for taste, curiosity, and
leisure" but aside from some Peale paintings, it largely was a con-
glomeration of curiosities, some worthy of note, some not. Displays
included fossil skeletons, stuffed animals, live animals, a tattooed
head, a mummified man and a mummified cat, a number of
Indian headdresses, and a knife with 98 blades.[6] Over the years
many such museums appeared for brief periods, with the emphasis
increasingly on freaks in nature, genuine and contrived. The best
known of the side-show museums was P. T. Barnum's American
Museum, which was established in New York in 1842. Its attrac-
tions included a pair of Siamese twins; General Tom Thumb, the
famous midget; and the Fiji Mermaid, the upper half of a monkey
joined to the lower half of a fish.

The Pennsylvania Academy of the Fine Arts, on the other hand,
was a serious, if somewhat stuffy, museum which largely grew out
of the interest of well-to-do amateurs. Many museums that survive
today had similar origins. Amateurs attracted by the arts, history,
or science would form a society where they could jointly pursue
their interest. Often a museum would result. The Charleston

---

[6] Herbert and Marjorie Katz, *Museums U.S.A.: A History and Guide*. New
York: Doubleday & Company, Inc., 1965, p. 13.

Museum was the earliest of a goodly number established in this way in the years before the Civil War. Some others were the Peabody Museum of Salem, Massachusetts (1799), the New-York Historical Society (1804), the Academy of Natural Sciences in Philadelphia (1812), the Society of Natural History in Boston, ancestor of today's Museum of Science (1830), the California Academy of Sciences (1853), and the Chicago Historical Society (1856).

The Smithsonian Institution was also founded in this period amid rather peculiar circumstances. In 1835 Congress learned that a wealthy English scientist, James Smithson, had left the United States Government a bequest of 100,000 pounds or, at existing values, $508,318.46. The money was to be used to organize "an establishment for the increase and diffusion of knowledge among men." What puzzled Congress was that (1) somebody would *want* to give money, (2) he was a foreigner, (3) he had never been to the United States, and (4) he didn't know any Ameicans.[7] To confuse things even more, Smithson didn't explain what kind of an "establishment" he had in mind. Some Congressmen wanted to refuse the offer, but others didn't agree. After three years of debate it was decided to accept the money and in 1838 a messenger was dispatched to England for that purpose. He returned with 105 bags of gold sovereigns which promptly were deposited in the U.S. Treasury. But the question of what kind of establishment would be organized remained unsettled.

In 1846 Congress finally made up its mind. The Smithsonian Institution would serve as a museum, a chemical laboratory, a reference collection of scientific materials, an art gallery, and a library. It also would have lecture rooms. Congress then appointed a board of regents to oversee things. It consisted, as it does today, of the Chief Justice of the United States, the Vice President, three Senators, three Representatives, and six private citizens. The fol-

---

[7] However, his half brother, Lord Percy, was the British officer in charge at the Battle of Lexington.

lowing year the Smithsonian began operations under the direction of Joseph Henry, a former Princeton University science professor. In 1855, the Smithsonian's first building in Washington was opened, the red stone castle on the Mall that to this day serves as administrative headquarters. Three years later a small display was established from which has sprung the world's greatest complex of museums.[8]

Before the turn of the century, five more of the nation's major museums had been established—The American Museum of Natural History in New York and the Art Institute of Chicago (1869), the Metropolitan Museum of Art (1870), the Museum of Fine Arts in Boston (1876), and Chicago's Field Museum of Natural History (1893). In addition, in 1899, the first children's museum was opened in Brooklyn, New York. In 1921 the National Park Service opened in Yosemite National Park the first of scores of trailside museums whose purpose was to explain the significance of various natural areas throughout the country.

The 1920's and 1930's also saw a great revival of interest in the nation's historical heritage. In 1927 Colonial Williamsburg was established in Virginia. By 1930 the Henry Ford Museum and Greenfield Village were in operation in Dearborn, Michigan. In this period the Federal government began a major program to improve preservation of the nation's historic sites. Its first step was to give the National Park Service responsibility for preserving the most important and developing museums at each. In 1933 the first two science and industry museums opened their doors, the Museum of Science and Industry in Chicago and the Franklin Institute in Philadelphia. With the country beset by a great economic depression, however, and then by war, there were few other

[8] Today the Smithsonian includes the National Museum, which oversees the Museum of History and Technology and the Museum of Natural History; the National Air Museum; the National Gallery of Art; the Freer Gallery of Art; the National Collection of Fine Arts; and the National Portrait Gallery. In addition, a museum to house the Joseph Hirshhorn collection of American art is planned.

changes until peace returned. Then, as we have seen, there were a great many.

Of the 5,000 museums in operation today about half are concerned with history. The remainder are divided more or less equally between art and science. Some museums, called general museums, try to deal with all three fields. New Jersey's leading museums, the Newark Museum and the state museum, are in this category. However, the largest number specialize either in art, history, or science. A major museum tries to deal with all aspects of its field. Through its collections, for example, the Metropolitan Museum of Art in New York attempts to provide a survey of the history of art over 7,000 years. The Field Museum of Natural History and the American Museum of Natural History try to do the same thing in the natural sciences, maintaining collections that cover as many areas as possible of this broad subject. The Smithsonian's vast Museum of History and Technology assumes a similar role with the history of the United States. Of course, the smaller a museum, the more difficult it is for it to cover a broad subject in detail. As a result, most select a limited area to concentrate on. Some deal with the history of a state, as the Minnesota Historical Society in St. Paul does, or a region within a state, as the New York State Historical Association in Cooperstown does, or a city, as the Atwater Kent Museum in Philadelphia does, or a town, as the Historical Society of Princeton, New Jersey, does. In other cases, the focus might be transportation as at the Baltimore & Ohio Railroad Museum in Baltimore, or industry as at the Hagley Museum outside Wilmington, Delaware, or Indians as at the Museum of the Plains Indian in Browning, Montana. There are hundreds of examples one might offer.

WHO OWNS MUSEUMS?

Two-thirds of American museums are privately owned. Of these, a small proportion are businesses organized to make a profit. Generally, they are run by one or two individuals. Mrs. Wilkerson's Figure Bottle Museum in Camdenton, Missouri, is an example;

the Edward-Dean Museum of Decorative Arts in Beaumont, California, is another. A few are relatively large businesses such as the National Historical Museum, Inc., of Washington, D.C., which operates a chain of wax museums. There also are museums which have been set up by manufacturing companies, banks, and other firms. Such museums do not earn income, but may improve a company's reputation and thereby help to improve its profits. Some company museums are very good, such as the history room at the Wells Fargo Bank in San Francisco and the Crane Company's museum of papermaking in Dalton, Massachusetts. Sometimes a company will organize a foundation to support a museum so that the museum will have independence in its activities and perhaps achieve greater status. The highly regarded Hagley Museum was endowed in this way by the du Pont Company.

Most privately owned museums, on the other hand, are owned by nonprofit corporations formed by private citizens for the sole purpose of operating such an institution. For example, nonprofit corporations operate the Metropolitan Museum of Art, the American Museum of Natural History, the Science Museum in St. Paul, Minnesota, and George Washington's home at Mount Vernon, Virginia. At times, a nonprofit organization will operate a museum as just one of its activities. This is the case with historical societies and also with some universities and colleges. Of course, museums also are owned by governments, as, for example, those museums operated by the Smithsonian Institution and the National Park Service, under the Federal government. Many states also maintain museums. Generally these tell something of what their state is like, but they differ widely in their approaches. In Illinois the state museum concentrates on natural history; in Virginia it functions as a museum of fine arts and a statewide center for the performing arts. There also are county-owned museums, such as the natural history and art museums in Los Angeles, and there are museums owned by cities, such as the City Art Museum of St. Louis and the Milwaukee Public Museum. In some situations, a government and a nonprofit corporation will share responsibility for a museum. For example, although the American Museum of Natural History and a number of other museums in New York are privately owned, the buildings they occupy are owned and maintained by the city. This also is the case with the Philadelphia Museum of Art.

HOW MUSEUMS ARE ORGANIZED

Ordinarily a nonprofit museum is governed by a board of trustees. The board, in turn, selects a director to operate the museum. The director selects the staff. If a museum is publicly owned, the trustees usually are appointed by the government involved. If the museum is privately owned, the board appoints new members itself. In both cases, trustees are appointed for a set number of years, often three or five, and serve without pay. Trustees are selected for a number of reasons. Some are asked to serve because of special knowledge they will bring to the board. For example, art museums like to have at least a few collectors as trustees, just as science museums seek trustees from the scientific community. Lawyers and financial experts often are selected because of the advice they can provide. Others are chosen for their leadership abilities or for influence they have which would be useful in furthering the interests of the museum. Frequently such persons are members of the local establishment that helps get things done in a city or a town. They may include corporation executives, businessmen, lawyers, educators, clubwomen, and members of prominent families. Often trustees also are chosen because they are wealthy and perhaps will give a large gift to the museum. As one museum director explained, "One doesn't have to be rich to be a trustee, but it helps."

One of the primary jobs of a board of trustees is to develop the broad policies which determine how a museum is run and the direction in which it moves. This takes in finances, personnel, operating procedures and, in the case of art museums, acquisitions. A board's other major responsibility is helping to raise money for the museum. Boards range in size from as few as ten members to as many as forty, but largely their work is done through committees: an executive committee which may be empowered to make decisions; a finance committee, which is concerned with investments and budget; and, at times, an acquisitions committee, which approves all additions to the museum's collections. A capable board of trustees can make the difference between an average museum and a superior museum. On the other hand, a board that oversteps its responsibilities and interferes in day-to-day operations can have the opposite effect. It was just such a clash of authority that seriously disrupted the progress of the new $12 million Los Angeles County Museum of Art and caused the resignation in 1965 of its director, Dr. Richard F. Brown.

Even under the best of circumstances, the job of a museum director is not an easy one. In the smallest museums he may do virtually everything: acquire collections, care for them, exhibit them, publicize the museum, and raise funds. In a larger museum he also wears many hats, but at least he has a staff to help him. Ordinarily a museum director oversees all the collecting, research, and exhibiting his museum does. As the museum's top administrator, he also deals with finances, labor relations, and legal problems. As the museum's top fund-raiser, he seeks contributions from all likely sources. As the museum's chief public representative and diplomat, he spends a good deal of time attending meetings, being interviewed, and, as one museum man explained, "smiling at old ladies, trustees, and others." So complicated has the job become that Chicago's Field Museum has as its director not a scientist but a professional administrator who also is a certified public accountant. At the Minneapolis Institute of Arts, two jobs have been created to deal with the problem. A former bank president handles administration, public relations, and fund-raising; and the director concerns himself with fine arts. But these are unusual arrangements.

In a small museum the staff may consist of just a handful of persons. At the Dayton Museum of Natural History, in Ohio, there are a director, a curator in charge of activities relating to

earth sciences, a curator of conservation and wildlife, a planetarium director, a director of children's work, three museum assistants, a secretary, and a custodian—or some ten full-time people.
In addition, there are about a half-dozen high school students who
serve as helpers after school and on weekends.

The larger a museum, the more extensive are its activities and
the more varied a staff it needs. The Museum of Fine Arts in
Boston, for example, is organized under an over-all director into
departments including Asiatic Art, Classical Art, Decorative Arts
and Sculpture, Egyptian Art, Paints, Prints and Drawings, and
Textiles. Each is staffed with curators and their assistants. Some
also have conservators whose task it is to restore and preserve
objects of great age and rarity. In addition, the museum has an
Education Department with a staff of instructors who conduct
lectures and classes and a team of specialists who produce educational television shows in the museum's galleries. Moreover, there
is a full-time school for art students. There also are librarians
who staff two libraries, editors who prepare publications, scientists
who operate a research laboratory in conservation techniques, a
photographer, the staff of the museum book shop and restaurant, a
superintendent of buildings and grounds and his many assistants, a
fund-raising expert who assists the director and the board of
trustees, a public relations expert, an exhibits designer, and a registrar who keeps records on all objects in the museum. In addition,
there are members of a business staff, guards, secretaries, clerks,
and other assistants—in all, over three hundred persons.

Even if it has no other specialists, a museum is likely to need
someone to serve as curator. A curator's job is as varied as that of
the director. One of his most important responsibilities is to
assemble collections and to care for them. In most cases he also
does research in his field and, when he finds time, publishes papers
so that other scholars may share in his findings. To keep up with
his field he also must read on his specialty and attend meetings. At
intervals he may spend a good deal of time planning and developing exhibits. He also may teach university courses, help graduate

students with their research, and even help high school students with their homework. Some curators write articles for popular magazines, give lectures, and speak on radio and television to acquaint the public with their work. Curators also answer an unending series of questions from children, adults, editors, writers, and businessmen. At museums of natural history, these questions often concern identification. People want to know what something is, whether it is dangerous, how old it is, and whether it is valuable. Sometimes they send their specimens to the museum for examination; occasionally they even bring them in.

The answers aren't always what the questioner hopes for. Bobb Schaeffer, a curator at the American Museum of Natural History, recalls a visit from a woman who came armed with a shopping bag full of what she thought were fossilized grasshoppers. When she dumped them on his table, he could see that these weren't fossils at all, but only long, thin, cigar-shaped pieces of rock. "When I told her this," he relates, "she looked at me for a minute, then asked, 'Isn't there an older staff member around here with more experience?'" Sometimes inquiries relate to careers. Sometimes free samples are requested—usually dinosaur bones.

At art museums and at some history museums curators also engage in what is known as "expertising." If you have a work of art you want to know more about, a curator will study it and tell you what he can. He will be able to tell you if it is good, bad, or indifferent. If necessary, he also may be able to tell you such things as its age and who the artist might be. However, he will not place a value on the work. At the National Gallery of Art in Washington art objects are examined by appointment each Wednesday from 9 to 11 and 3 to 5. In a recent year, 1,740 people took advantage of this service. It is offered in the registrar's office in a curtained area which has become known as the "fortuneteller's booth."

One of the serious problems facing museums is that curators and other museum personnel are in short supply. Every museum has the problem, from the smallest to the largest. One reason for the shortage has been the rapid increase in the number of museums.

Another is the low salaries museums pay. However, this is a matter of necessity rather than desire, since, as we shall see, most museums have a hard time making ends meet. As a result of their limited funds, most rely heavily on unpaid volunteer help. Over fifty thousand persons throughout the nation contribute their services. In many museums, particularly art museums, volunteers serve as guides for visiting school children and adults. In fact, education programs at most museums would not be possible without volunteers. At the Art Institute of Chicago there are over one hundred volunteer teachers to supplement a paid education staff of twenty-one. At the National Gallery of Art in Washington, D.C., there are 150. But volunteers also serve in many other ways. At Boston's Museum of Science young people help care for the live animals displayed, work in the museum shop, do clerical work, and polish a huge lighthouse lens that the museum owns. At the Oregon Historical Society's museum in Portland, volunteers mend costumes, do photography, and often contribute special knowledge on problems the curator must deal with. At the Los Angeles County Museum of Natural History, three volunteers collect insects for the Entymology Department. At the Dossin Great Lakes Museum in Detroit, volunteers build intricate scale models of ships for display, spending months or even years on a single model. In some museums volunteers serve as receptionists, switchboard operators, typists, catalogers, fund-raisers, and, in a few cases, as part-time curators.

HOW MUSEUMS ARE FINANCED

Running a museum these days is very costly. In a recent year, for example, these museums spent the following amounts:

Seattle Art Museum, $137,102; The Science Museum, Saint Paul, $158,998; Cranbrook Institute of Science, Bloomfield Hills, Michigan, $208,445; Detroit History Museums, $342,611; City Art Museum of St. Louis, $925,103; California Academy of Sciences, San Francisco, $1,352,033; Sturbridge Village, Sturbridge, Massachusetts, $1,568,171; Field Museum, Chicago, $2,565,236; Metropolitan Museum of Art, New York, $5,278,279.

These amounts may seem large, but there are many expenses that people not associated with museums are inclined to overlook. To get a sense of what is involved, consider some of the operating expenses in the budget of the medium-sized City Art Museum of St. Louis. Costs of the sort listed below confront all museums:

Salaries and wages	$368,059.50
Social Security taxes	11,271.01
Pension	14,388.46
Publicity, advertising	14,592.28
Office, administrative expense	38,131.89
Insurance premiums	19,102.56
Light, heat, power	16,671.03
Repairs, maintenance of building	20,001.55
Building improvements	13,171.67
New equipment	9,343.97
Special exhibitions	28,992.17
Transportation of art objects, traveling and moving expenses	5,839.48
Exhibit installation, gallery redecoration	13,295.25
Conservation, curatorial expense	2,338.41
Books, periodicals for library	5,152.39
Printing of publications	5,343.97
Auditorium lectures, programs	3,007.95

To fully understand such figures, it is important to recognize that they are minimum expenditures, that the museum could have spent considerably more on each of these items without being extravagant. Indeed, the problem is that most museums are not spending enough, particularly on salaries, on caring for their collections, on maintaining and expanding their buildings, and on scholarly research and publication. They don't spend enough simply because they don't have enough. This is an old problem, but a number of developments have made it even more difficult. One such development has been the great increase in attendance, which has placed extraordinary demands on museums. Another has been the growing use of museums by schools and the development of costly education programs. Still another is that everything is more expensive these days. Related to this is the fact that museum income isn't growing fast enough to keep up.

A number of museum people complain that the public doesn't realize that most museums need contributions to meet expenses. They are particularly disturbed by persons from the suburbs who use big city museums and do nothing to help support them. Even more important, they say, is that governments and foundations have not given museums enough financial support. In response to more aggressive lobbying by museum officials, the Federal government and some state governments have begun to increase their contributions. The Federal government also has begun to help in other ways. A few weeks before this was written the National Museum Act was signed into law. It directs the Smithsonian Institution to work with museums in training personnel and improving their operations. However, all this is but a step in the right direction. Most museums continue to have a hard time meeting expenses.[9]

Where do museums obtain their money? There are four sources: investment and gifts, government agencies, admission and membership fees, and businesses museums operate. The importance of each varies from museum to museum.

In a recent year, for example, the privately owned Seattle Art Museum had an operating budget of almost $140,000. One-third of the funds came from investment income; another third came from membership fees; and the remainder was derived from gifts and from sales at the museum's retail shop. At the publicly owned City Art Museum in St. Louis that year the budget was about one million dollars. Two-thirds of the money needed came from taxes; the rest came from contributions and museum shop sales. At

[9] Museums with reasonably comfortable incomes include the Smithsonian complex, the Metropolitan Museum of Art in New York, the Cleveland Museum of Art, the Isabella Stewart Gardner Museum in Boston, and the Sterling and Francine Clark Art Institute in Williamstown, Massachusetts.

the privately operated Field Museum of Natural History in Chicago the budget was two million dollars. Investment income provided about half of what was needed. Gifts, research grants, and a contribution from the city made up the rest.

Investments. One museum in four in the United States owns securities or real estate which produces income each year. Such investments are known as "endowment." The funds involved usually are gifts that have been received over the years. A few museums have very large endowments. The endowment funds at the Metropolitan Museum of Art in New York have a value of over $100 million. They are the largest of any American museum, earning some $4 million a year or about 60 per cent of what the Metropolitan needs for its operations. The investments of the Cleveland Museum of Art have a value of over $70 million, earning some $3 million a year. But these are unusual situations. At the California Academy of Sciences in San Francisco investment income amounts to about $200,000 a year or about 20 per cent of expenses. At the far smaller Dayton Museum of Natural History in Ohio, income from investments in a recent year came to $911.13. Three museums in four have no investment income.

Gifts. At times a person will give a museum cash, securities, or valuable objects because he has decided on his own that the museum is a worthwhile institution. More often a museum must seek out the gifts that come to it. Two of the museums I visited in Boston were in the throes of major fund-raising drives. The Museum of Fine Arts was trying to raise $13.4 million in gifts primarily to expand its building and increase salaries. The Museum of Science was attempting to raise $8 million to build a new wing. Some years ago New York's Museum of Modern Art collected $25 million to expand its building in the largest fund-raising drive ever carried out by a museum. Contributions came from 3,000 people in 43 states and 15 countries. However, these efforts were special campaigns to pay for construction of new facilities. To obtain money for operating expenses and, at times, for acquisitions, most museums also try to raise funds on a continuing basis. Traditionally they have turned to wealthy individuals. In recent years business corporations also have been asked to help. Of course not all requests for funds are granted. On the other hand, some gifts may be very generous. The director of a major science museum told me with quiet pleasure of raising $1.5 million simply by writing a letter.

To help their directors and trustees obtain contributions, a number of privately owned museums have added professional fund-raisers to their staffs. To supplement what they get in government funds, several publicly owned museums rely on special fund-raising organizations set up by their supporters. The most successful of these is the Founders Society of the Detroit Institute of Arts. In a ten-year period it raised almost $16 million for art works, education programs, a music series, a puppet theatre, and other activities that funds from the city of Detroit did not cover.

Museums go about their fund-raising in many ways. Some receive help from volunteer groups such as the Friends of the City Art Museum in St. Louis which sponsors the annual Fine Arts Ball there. At the Oregon Museum of Science and Industry in Portland and at the Seattle Art Museum there are annual auctions that yield large sums. In raising money for its planetarium, Boston's Museum of Science went so far as to sell the sky. The sun was priced at $10,000; a star in the Milky Way cost a dollar. Each purchaser received a deed to his "property." The idea netted the museum $150,000.

Government Funds. One American museum in three is operated by a government agency and receives at least its basic expenses from the taxpayers. However, as we have seen, such a museum often must turn elsewhere for additional money. Some privately operated museums also get financial help from cities and towns they serve, mostly for maintenance of their buildings. Of course, another source of government aid these days is the Federal government. Most of the established natural history museums receive sizable sums for their research projects from agencies such as the National Science Foundation, the Atomic Energy Commission, the National Institute of Health, and the United States Defense Department. In addition, a growing number of museums receive Federal assistance for their education programs.

Foundations. To date, relatively little help has come to the museums from the major foundations. The Ford Foundation pays for a program to train graduate students who plan to work in art museums. It also supports the preparation of scholarly catalogs which describe the collections in art museums. The Carnegie Corporation paid for an Artmobile, one of four traveling art galleries used by the Virginia Museum of Fine Arts in its education program. Together with the Sloan Foundation, it covered the cost of a mathematics classroom and library at the Pacific Science Center in Seattle. Otherwise, the help that museums receive from this source comes from little-known foundations operated by wealthy families. The Hill Foundation of Minneapolis, for example, has given generous sums to the Oregon Museum of Science and Industry and The Science Museum in Saint Paul, just as the Countway Foundation has helped the Museum of Science in Boston.

Membership Fees. Some people have the impression that one must be a member of high society to join a museum. Nothing could be farther from the truth. Museums want as many members as they can get. Members represent income and community support. All one needs to join a museum is the price of a membership, usually $10 to $20 a year for families, and far less for young people. In turn, a member receives free admissions where fees are charged, discounts on purchases at the museum shop, advance notice on what's going on, a chance to see exhibits before the public does, and occasional invitations to social affairs. The art museums have been particularly successful in attracting members. The largest museum membership in the United States is at the Museum of Modern Art in New York, where some forty thousand members pay in a half million dollars a year in fees, or about 15 per cent of the museum budget. About one museum in four also charges an admission fee. Others charge fees for special exhibits, courses, lectures, and workshops.

Business Ventures. Many museums try to increase their income by operating businesses. Typically a museum, or a group of volunteers, will operate a retail shop where publications and other materials relating to the museum are sold. In shops at art museums one can buy reproductions of art works and occasionally rent or

Members of the Founders Society of the Detroit Institute of Arts celebrate the opening of a new museum wing. *Courtesy Detroit Institute of Arts*

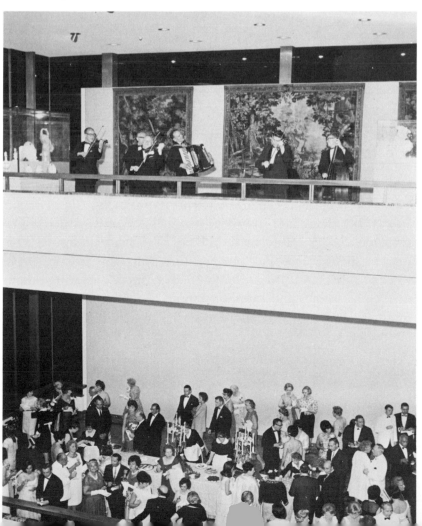

buy originals. Also Christmas cards, copies of ancient art objects, and even toys may be available. At George Washington's home in Mount Vernon, Virginia, the museum shop sells slips of boxwood from shrubs Washington planted almost two centuries ago. At Colonial Williamsburg, one may buy leather belts, silver coffee pots and other articles created by craftsmen in demonstrating how things were done in Colonial days. Moreover, commercial firms pay for permission to reproduce and sell furniture, wallpaper, paint, and other items used at the museum. At Old Sturbridge Village in Sturbridge, Massachusetts, sales of merchandise in four museum shops came to over $700,000 in a recent year, which was almost half the museum's income. Sales of books and souvenirs at the Chicago Museum of Science and Industry amounted to $1.5 million in the same period. However, most museum shops operate at the other end of the scale with sales that range between $10,000 and $20,000, and not all make a profit.

Museums also are in the publications business, producing books, magazines, guides, and other items they sell. One of the biggest such ventures is conducted by the Museum of Modern Art in New York, which has published over a hundred books that earn as much as half a million dollars a year. Another involves the American Museum of Natural History, which publishes the magazine *Natural History* (circulation 175,000) and, with Doubleday and Company, issues many books.

There are museums that sell science equipment. The Oregon Museum of Science and Industry assembles and sells science kits to the schools. The California Academy of Sciences manufactures Foucault Pendulums and planetarium units for sale to other museums. Museums also are in the food business, operating restaurants, coffee shops, and cafeterias, some of which are very good, but others, alas, which are only convenient.[10]

---

[10] Three of the best are the Polynesian restaurant at the Gallery of Modern Art in New York, the handsome cafeteria around an indoor pool at the Metropolitan Museum of Art, and the dining room at the Museum of Fine Arts in Boston.

A discussion of this sort may leave one with the impression that money pours into a museum's coffers from all directions. Of course this is not the case. Museums collect money wherever they can only because most do not have a single source of income that adequately meets their needs.

HOW MUSEUMS ARE PROTECTED

Although shortages of money and staff are the biggest problems for most museums, security is not far behind. Increases in vandalism and petty thievery have alarmed museum officials all over the United States. A curator at the Smithsonian told me, "More and more people come to the museum who see it as a place in which to run around and have fun. We would like to have lots of open exhibits people can examine at close range, but any that are not behind glass become a target and are in danger." His concern was echoed wherever I traveled. The problem has many forms. Often it involves "touching." Out of curiosity people thoughtlessly reach out to see what an irreplaceable painting feels like, with the result at times that the painting is damaged. Sculpture and armor also suffer in that touching literally wears them away. In other cases, the visitor knows perfectly well what he is doing. Some write on the walls or on valued objects, using lipstick or ink. Others take "souvenirs" such as the nuts, bolts, and raised letters they may find in displays. In search of more unusual trophies, some even leap barriers to enter period rooms of rare furniture or habitat groups of preserved animals. Still others deliberately punch holes in priceless canvases or slash them or attempt to break mechanical exhibits.

Museums try to deal with these problems in a variety of ways. A growing number display their valuables under glass. Museums also fasten down as much as they can. In art museums, furniture drawers may be fixed so they don't pull out; handles may be wired in place; vases and bowls may be secured with metal bands painted to blend with the object; still other treasures may be bolted to tables or pedestals. A number of museums also have alarms which go off if an object is moved or a barrier is hurdled. To discourage "touchers," the Guggenheim Museum in New York has installed "don't cross" lines in front of its paintings; others use velour-covered ropes. As a general measure, some museums have increased their guard forces. At least one, which can't afford more guards, uses civilian volunteers to patrol its galleries. The Metropolitan Museum of Art is outfitting its many guards with uniforms resembling those of the New York State Police. It is hoped that with a more military appearance the guards will command more respect. The New Jersey State Museum also has a sizable security force, but its philosophy is quite different. Most of its guards are motherly-looking women in well-tailored blazers. Why women? "When women smile," Museum Director Kenneth Prescott explained, "men smile and children listen." However, there are a few museums that do not have guards. Their reasoning is that guards serve, not as a deterrent, but as a challenge to a potential vandal who will want to see how much he can get away with.

Museums also must protect themselves against the theft of valuable objects. Over the years many have suffered serious losses at the hands of professional thieves or clever amateurs. A few days before my visit to the Chicago Historical Society a thief stole a rare 400-year-old book valued at over $20,000. In the months that followed paintings were taken from the Art Institute of Chicago and the Philadelphia Musum of Art. However, the most spectacular theft in recent years occurred at the American Museum of Natural History. On the night of October 29, 1964, thieves scaled a steep wall, entered the museum through a window, and escaped with twenty-two gems from the Morgan Hall of Gems and Minerals. Included in the theft were the priceless Star of India, which is the world's largest known sapphire, the DeLong Ruby, and the Midnight Star Sapphire. Fortunately, the thieves were caught and the major jewels recovered. When a theft does occur, museums generally follow a set procedure, reporting the loss to a number of agencies in the United States and abroad. Along with the police, they include dealers in the kind of object stolen, pawnshops, the

American Association of Museums, which notifies its membership, and magazines published for collectors.

To protect against such losses, museums use a wide variety of approaches. Most have guards on duty throughout the night who check in with the police on an established schedule from "stations" at various points in the building. At the Los Angeles County Museum of Natural History a watchdog accompanies the guards on their rounds. Museums also protect themselves with a variety of highly sophisticated electronic equipment. One of the most advanced systems is in operation at the new Los Angeles County Museum of Art. While TV cameras keep watch on each

A closed-circuit TV camera keeps watch in medieval art gallery at Los Angeles County Museum of Art. *Courtesy Honeywell, Inc.*

gallery, other devices listen for any sound, motion, or vibration in the building. The equipment is monitored at a central console from which an operator can contact any guard in the museum and automatically open and close any of the building's many doors. Should the system be tampered with, it is backed up by still another security system.[11]

A NOTE ON THE USE OF MUSEUMS

Advice on visiting different kinds of museums and looking at various kinds of exhibits is provided in the chapters that follow. The point to be made here is that most museums offer many opportunities for learning and pleasure. Looking at exhibits is but one. As we have seen, there also may be lectures, classes, workshops, concerts, films, and field trips, for young people as well as for adults. There also may be opportunities to learn more of how a museum operates by working as a volunteer or becoming involved in a junior curator program. In any case, the way to get to know a museum is to first learn something about it and then spend some time there exploring. Either write for material in advance, including a stamped, addressed envelope, or pick up what is available when you arrive and study it before you begin your visit. Ideally, you should have a map, something that briefly describes the collections, and a calendar of current activities. If possible, visit on a weekday since the museum will be less crowded then and plan to spend an hour or so looking around. Any longer than that is likely to leave your eyes and legs tired. If you decide it is the kind of place you would enjoy, come back often and make the museum yours. You are likely to have an interesting time.

[11] Tom Probst, Joseph M. Chapman, Albert J. Grossman, "Security and the Museum," Washington, D.C.: American Association of Museums.

2 | Art Muscums

ON AN AVERAGE DAY ABOUT SEVEN THOUSAND PEOPLE VISIT CHICAGO'S twenty-acre Art Institute. On one summer day when I was there, other visitors included children who had come to see the Junior Museum and be toured through one of the galleries, children who had come to take art courses, members of a class from the University of Wisconsin who had journeyed 150 miles to see and hear about certain paintings, some fifty adults who had assembled for a talk on the Flemish painters, and a group of blind men and women who had come to touch sculpture. However, most of the seven thousand visitors were on their own. Either they had come to see a particular collection or painting or object, or they had come with nothing more special in mind than seeking pleasure.

Whatever their reasons, there was much for them to see. Along with paintings and sculpture, the museum's one hundred galleries house prints and drawings, photographs, furniture, costumes, textiles, silverware and glassware, ceramics, metalwork and woodwork, primitive masks, and other rare and beautiful things men throughout the world have created over thousands of years. Perhaps the greatest of the museum's many treasures are its nineteenth and twentieth century paintings, particularly those by painters of the French Impressionist school; its 50,000 prints and drawings; its Chinese bronze sculptures; its 700-year-old Spanish altarpiece; and its 67 miniature period rooms each a cubic foot in size, each depicting a different example of interior design since the sixteenth century. In all, the Art Institute's possessions are worth hundreds of millions of dollars. Of far more importance, however, is the extraordinary picture they provide of man's aspirations, experiences, and talents. Although most of the artists represented are long dead, their work remains as a permanent record of what they experienced, what they saw in the lives of those around them, and what they regarded as beautiful or dreadful.

The Art Institute of Chicago is one of about a dozen major art museums in the United States. The largest in terms of its collections is the Metropolitan Museum of Art in New York. Other leading art museums include the Brooklyn Museum, the Museum of Modern Art, and the Whitney Museum of American Art, also in New York; the National Gallery of Art in Washington; the major art museums in Boston, Philadelphia, Detroit, Cleveland, Toledo, and Minneapolis; and the California Palace of the Legion of Honor in San Francisco.

Scattered throughout the country are another seven hundred art museums, usually with more limited collections, with smaller staffs, and with far less money to spend. Some concentrate on a particular field as do the Museum of Primitive Art and the Museum of Contemporary Crafts in New York. However, many are general art museums serving not only their home cities but large regions. The Seattle Art Museum is one example, drawing visitors and school groups from throughout the state of Washington. The Portland Art Museum 150 miles to the south of Seattle is another. It is the only art museum in all of Oregon to which large numbers of people can turn if they want to see original art of high quality. The museum is particularly well known for its collection of headdresses, masks, drums, and other folk art of the Northwest Indians. But it also possesses one of the collections of Italian Renaissance paintings that Samuel Kress, the dime-store millionaire, left to museums all over the country, and it has other treasures as well: a famous water-lily painting by Claude Monet (for which it spent more than it usually does on all its acquisitions in a single year), a painting by Pierre Auguste Renoir, other paintings by the Oregon artist C. F. Price, a group of Japanese prints, a sculpture by the modern artist Constantin Brancusi, and some handsome English silverware. But the overall collection is small. While a visitor would need many days to see everything on display at the Art Institute of Chicago, he probably could see Portland's offerings in an afternoon. Of course, there also are other differences. Compared with Chicago's budget of $4,000,000 a year, Portland's is but $300,000. While the Art Institute may spend upwards of $800,000 a year on art works, the Portland museum may spend but $50,000 a year; while Chicago has a staff of 300, Portland has a staff of 15. Yet in a city of only 400,000 people, Portland's art museum attracts at least 100,000 visitors every year.

The nation's art museums include a large number that are far smaller than the one in Portland. Many are products of the cultural explosion discussed in the preceding chapter. Often they serve not only as museums, but as community art centers, offering courses, performances, and workshops, as well as exhibits. Lacking collections of good quality and also the money for them, they rely largely on traveling exhibits they rent or borrow from other museums.

When the now giant Metropolitan Museum of Art was founded

in 1870 its objectives were to "encourage and develop the study
of fine arts and the application of arts to . . . practical life"
and then to "advance the general knowledge . . . and popular
instruction." Whether an art museum is large or small, these
century-old objectives still apply. The only differences between
then and now are that far more people are involved and that
museums are actively seeking a mass audience, not just going
through the motions. In 1965, there were 45 million visits to art
museums and art centers. Of course, the extent to which art
museums actually advance "the general knowledge . . . and
popular instruction" is more difficult to measure. Even museum
people acknowledge that at this point they are not sure.

A HISTORY OF GIFTS

Eighty per cent of the Metropolitan Museum of Art's holdings
have come to it through gift or bequest. It is the same with most
art museums in the United States. Virtually all of what they have
either has been given to them by private collectors or purchased
by them with gifts of cash. The collectors have had the more
dramatic impact. Indeed, much of the history of American art
museums can be told in terms of enormously wealthy tycoons and
society figures who assembled rare and beautiful art works from all
over the world, sometimes in wholesale lots, then either gave or
left them to museums, or established museums for them. They
collected for various reasons. After making millions, some decided
that money wasn't enough and sought refinement and tranquillity
through contact with beauty. Others loved the objects they
acquired. Still others came to love collecting for its own sake and
compulsively acquired more and more and more. Some turned
their possessions over to museums to benefit the public. Others
were in search of immortality. What better way to be pleasantly
remembered than to have a museum named after you? In more
recent years, of course, tax deductions for such gifts also have come
to play a role. J. Pierpont Morgan, financier and founder of U.S.
Steel; Charles Lang Freer, a manufacturer of railroad cars;

Andrew Mellon, the investment banker; more recently, his son Paul, a philanthropist; and Samuel H. Kress, founder of the Kress dime-store chain—these are but a few collectors who have bestowed greatness on museums. In Europe, by contrast, many of the principal collectors were governments and kings, whose art works often were obtained over the centuries through the plunder of war.

The very wealthy did not begin to have their great impact on American art museums until after the Civil War when the nation developed a strong taste for art and people with money found it fashionable and exciting to travel abroad in search of paintings. However, the first museum in the United States in which art was displayed was opened many years earlier in 1784. As we have seen, it was the museum the portrait painter Charles Willson Peale established in his Philadelphia home and later moved to Independence Hall. Three hundred paintings by Peale and his son Rembrandt were shown. When Peale died in 1827, the museum was closed and the collection was scattered. In recent years the Federal government has reassembled a hundred Peale portraits at Independence National Historical Park in Philadelphia where they are displayed in Congress Hall next door to their old home at Independence Hall.

The nation's oldest existing art museum, the Pennsylvania Academy of the Fine Arts, at Broad and Cherry streets in Philadelphia, held its first exhibit in 1807. It consisted of paintings of Shakespearean scenes by Benjamin West, an American painter who lived in Europe, and plaster casts of statues in the Louvre museum in Paris. In 1831 Yale established the first university art museum in the United States when it purchased from Colonel John Trumbull his paintings of Revolutionary war scenes and established the Trumbull Gallery in New Haven, Connecticut.

In 1844 another American art museum of note came into being when the Wadsworth Atheneum was opened in Hartford, Connecticut. Just two years later, with the founding of the Smithsonian Institution, the Federal government gave official notice of its interest in art. The Smithsonian, it was decided by Congress, was to have a "gallery of art." But it was more easily decreed than done. In fact, four years later, the Smithsonian's assistant secretary lamented: "The formation of a gallery of the best paintings is, in this country, almost hopeless."[1] With little government money available for purchases, with no one willing to provide paintings or gifts of cash, by the 1860's all the gallery had assembled were thirty-eight cheap plaster casts of statues. Meanwhile, in New York, a well-to-do wholesale grocer named Lumin Reed had begun buying works of American artists in great numbers, becoming so involved that he transformed the third floor of his home into the New York Gallery of Fine Arts. After he died, the gallery was closed, and his paintings went to the New-York Historical Society, but Reed's place as the first major collector of American art was secure.

The great American art museums finally began to take shape in the 1860's and 1870's. That period saw the establishment of the Art Institute of Chicago, the Metropolitan Museum of Art in New York, the Museum of Fine Arts in Boston, and the Fine Arts Academy in Buffalo. The Metropolitan Museum originated in Paris with a committee. John Jay, grandson of the first chief justice of the United States, proposed the idea in 1866 to a group of Americans who had come together for a July Fourth celebration. Since many belonged to the influential Union League Club in New York, they wrote the club and urged it to take on formation of the museum as a project. The club agreed and in 1870 the Metropolitan was chartered. In 1872 it opened in rented quarters at 681 Fifth Avenue with 174 European paintings it had purchased with $106,000 in gifts. Once the museum was established, the gifts grew in number and magnificence, enabling the Metropolitan to quickly rise to its position among the finest art museums in the world. Among its hundreds of wealthy patrons over the years, three of the most lavish in their generosity were

---

[1] Walter Karp, "The Smithsonian Institution," New York: *American Heritage,* 1965, p. 96.

J. Pierpont Morgan, who left the museum over six thousand paintings, tapestries, porcelains, and sculptures worth more than $30 million and also was responsible for much of the museum's remarkable Egyptian collection; the H. O. Havemeyers, sugar millionaires, who willed the museum almost two thousand works of art; and John D. Rockefeller, Jr., whose supreme gift, among many gifts, was The Cloisters, a $60 million museum of medieval art, a tranquil place comprised of portions of five ancient monasteries brought together atop a bluff high above the Hudson River at the northern end of Manhattan Island.

During the 1870's William Walters, a Baltimore railroad man who founded the Atlantic Coast Line, and T. B. Walker, a Minneapolis lumberman, opened their homes to the public to show the art treasures they had assembled, much as Lumin Reed and Charles Willson Peale had done. In both cities, permanent museums resulted: in Baltimore, the charming, cluttered Walters Art Gallery; in Minneapolis, the Walker Art Center.

During the 1890's Isabella Stewart Gardner, a lively Boston society matron, began collecting art treasures for what was to become one of the loveliest museums in the country. With $3 million she had inherited and the advice of the famed art critic Bernard Berenson, she assembled extraordinary paintings, sculptures, tapestries, and furnishings, along with doors, archways, staircases, and columns. The building that houses these treasures was a copy of a beautiful fifteenth century Italian palace, the Palazzo Bardini on the Grand Canal in Venice. Even before its completion in 1902, the words "Isabella Stewart Gardner Museum" had been cut in the stone above the front door. However, it was not until after Mrs. Gardner's death in 1924 that the building would serve as a museum. Before this time she lived in the palace and perfected it. By the terms of her will, it was to remain just as she left it, with nothing added and nothing taken away. When she died her body lay in state, with lighted candles at her sides and a cross at her feet, in a part of the palace built from a Spanish cloister. For three days and three nights nuns prayed for her. Then the museum was opened. Today John Sargent's portrait of Mrs. Gardner hangs in the Gothic Room. On each April 14, her birthday, an Anglican mass is celebrated in the chapel. Four afternoons each week there is chamber music.[2]

The Phillips Collection in Washington, D.C., is another highly personal museum, the result of the efforts of Duncan and Marjorie Phillips. Other such museums are the Frick Collection, housed in the Fifth Avenue mansion of the late Henry Clay Frick, and the Seattle Art Museum, which has its roots in the collection of Oriental art gathered by a courtly geologist named Richard Fuller and his mother. In 1933 the Fullers gave the people of Seattle their art treasures and a museum to house them. In turn, Dr. Fuller became president of the museum and its director.

About the time Mrs. Gardner was building her Venetian palace in Boston, a totally different kind of museum was taking shape in Toledo, Ohio. Two men were involved. One was Edward Drummond Libby, the glass manufacturer. The other was George W. Stevens, newspaper reporter, writer, promotion man, poet, and artist. Both shared a single idea: to create a museum that would be a community enterprise, that all the people would support, and that all the people would turn to for education and enjoyment. Libby organized the museum in 1901. He rented quarters, hired a secretary, acquired fifteen trustees, twelve hundred members, a mummified cat and a painting, and held exhibitions of sorts. But enthusiasm soon died and Libby called in Stevens to take over as director. Along with the cat and the painting, Stevens inherited assets of $293. One of the first things he did was announce free drawing classes for children and adults, and free talks on art to school classes and anyone else who wanted them. He also announced that children were welcome in the museum even if they came without adults. He also made a speech. "The first thing I want to do," he said, "is remove from the minds of the people that

[2] Aline Saarinen, *The Proud Possessors,* New York: Random House, 1958, pp. 22–25; Katz, *Museums U.S.A.,* p. 55.

The 1,000-handed Kuan Yin, part of a major collection of Oriental art assembled by Richard Fuller, a Seattle geologist, and his mother. The collection was a gift to the Seattle Art Museum. *Courtesy Seattle Art Museum*

the Toledo Museum of Art is an ultraconservative association or an expensive luxury. It is neither one nor the other. It has something to give that all the people want and we want them all with us." Attendance began to rise, financial support began to increase, and the collection began to grow. The first section of the museum was completed in 1912. Libby paid half and the people contributed the rest in dimes and dollars. When more space was needed, again they shared the responsibility.

The early years of this century also saw the Federal government at last become seriously involved in the operation of art museums. In 1906 the "National Gallery" which the Congress had established sixty years earlier with the Smithsonian Institution and then proceeded to forget was revived when Harriet Lane Johnson, a niece of former President Buchanan, left it her collection of English masterpieces. The result was that space for the gallery was provided in the Smithsonian's Natural History Museum. In the same period, however, the Smithsonian accepted another gift. It was a remarkable collection of Oriental and American art, including most of the important work of the American artist James Whistler. Funds for a museum to house the collection also were provided. The donor was as remarkable as his gift. He was Charles Lang Freer who having made his many millions retired at forty-eight to do what he liked best: collect art. In 1923, four years after his death, the lovely Freer Gallery was opened in Washington.

Four years later, in 1927, Andrew Mellon, the investment banker, Secretary of the Treasury, and art collector, quietly began assembling paintings he hoped would form the nucleus of a truly great national art gallery. His objective was to bring together the very finest works. Even for a man such as Mellon with a personal fortune of over $500 million at his disposal, this was not an easy task. Working through the noted art dealers Knoedler and Company and Sir Joseph Duveen, Mellon slowly and carefully amassed 115 paintings and a number of sculptures, for which he paid over $30 million. Included in this group were twenty-one supreme masterpieces he purchased sight unseen from Leningrad's famed Hermitage Museum when the new Communist government, in desperate need of funds, decided that art was not quite as important as gold. Also included were forty-two works he purchased in one transaction from Duveen for $21 million, the largest single purchase of art ever made. On December 22, 1936, Mellon announced his gift in a letter to President Franklin Roosevelt. In addition to the $30 million in art works, he offered to provide $15 million for a museum and an endowment of still another $5 million to help meet the museum's expenses. Four days later, President Roosevelt accepted the offer and soon after so did Congress. It was the largest gift ever made by one person to a government. But it was not a total surprise. In 1934, the government had sued Mellon for nonpayment of over $3 million in income taxes. His defense was that the money had been spent on art works that were intended for the government. However, the trial dragged on and it was not until after his death in 1937 that he was found innocent. Soon after Mellon made his gifts, Joseph Widener, a Philadelphia millionaire, and Samuel H. Kress contributed their splendid collections of art works. In 1941 the National Gallery of Art was opened, occupying one of the largest and most beautiful marble buildings in the world. Two more important collections were to be added in succeeding years: the French Impressionist paintings collected and contributed by Chester Dale, an investment banker, and a collection of prints and drawings from Lessing Rosenwald, former chairman of Sears, Roebuck & Co., whose father, Julius Rosenwald, had launched the Chicago Museum of Science and Industry in the 1920's.

Over the years Samuel Kress continued to collect in behalf of the National Gallery of Art, and after his death his brother Rush did so, with the close guidance of the Gallery's staff. However, the Kress material became so vast that much of it could not be shown at the Gallery and was disbursed to other museums. It was in this way that art museums in eighteen cities where there were Kress stores acquired rich collections of paintings they could have obtained in no other way.[3]

Meanwhile, what had happened to the old National Gallery in the Natural History Museum? Today, it has a new name—the National Collection of Fine Arts; a new home—in an old building the Patent Office once occupied; and the ambitious assignment of encouraging the growth of art in America. It shares its headquarters with still another Smithsonian museum, the National Portrait Gallery, which was established in 1962 to bring together paintings and other illustrations of persons who had a significant role in American history. Here too gifts are crucial to the museum's growth.

The newest Federal art museum is being designed as this is written. Also a Smithsonian unit, it is to house 4,000 American paintings and 1,600 pieces of American sculpture valued at between $25 million and $50 million, a collection which has been brought together over the years by Joseph Hirshhorn, a son of poor immigrants who made his fortune in uranium. Although collectors sometimes seek museums to accept their gifts, more often it is the other way around. Certainly this was the case with the Hirshhorn collection. In this instance, however, it was governments, not museums, that were involved. Hirshhorn's original plan was to house his art works in a Canadian mining town he wanted to build and name after himself. When the mining town nearest the site he had chosen announced it wasn't interested in the business competition another community would offer, he dropped the idea. Later, British officials approached him and proposed to build a museum in London for his art works. At about the same time, Israel suggested a museum *it* would built in Jerusalem. Soon after, Los Angeles and Beverly Hills both announced their interest. Then New York State indicated its interest through Governor

[3] Allentown, Pennsylvania; Atlanta, Georgia; Birmingham, Alabama; Columbia, South Carolina; Denver; El Paso; Honolulu; Houston; Kansas City, Missouri; Memphis; Miami; New Orleans; Portland, Oregon; Raleigh, North Carolina; San Francisco; Seattle; Tucson; Tulsa.

Nelson Rockefeller, an important collector in his own right. Finally, President Johnson prevailed on Mr. Hirshhorn to give the collection to the people of the United States and he agreed.

Art museums of all sizes continue to grow through the generosity of the private collector, even though art works become more and more costly and, in the case of old masterpieces, become harder and harder to obtain. As we have seen, some gifts are princely. Thus, the usefulness and importance of San Francisco's De Young Museum was increased manyfold when it received from Avery Brundage, a Chicago businessman, a gift of $30 million in Oriental art he spent years in assembling. However, most gifts that art museums receive are far more modest. In a recent year, for example, the art museum in Portland, Oregon, was given a total of twenty-two art works by twelve donors, ranging from a 500-year-old Costa Rican bell donated by Mr. and Mrs. Robert Campbell of Portland to "Desert Scene with Bird," a Japanese print donated by Mrs. Harvey Slatin of New York. At the City Museum in St. Louis that year there were 25 donors; at the Minneapolis Institute of Arts, 29; at the far larger Art Institute of Chicago, 184; at New York's Museum of Modern Art, 289. However, not all gifts are accepted; in fact, with a museum's concern for quality, far more are turned down than accepted. Of course, occasionally politics may play a part, particularly in smaller, newer museums with bare walls and empty pocketbooks. As John Canaday, art critic of the New York *Times*, has noted, "There always is a chance that if you will accept the obviously phony Rembrandt from old Mrs. Gizzle . . . she will leave you some money if she ever dies. . . ."

Gifts for Purchases. In a typical year, the major art museums will spend several million dollars on art works. In 1965, for example, the Metropolitan Museum spent about $2 million; the Art Institute of Chicago, about $800,000; the Minneapolis Institute of Arts, about $300,000; the Seattle Museum of Art, between $50,000 and $100,000. Of course, most smaller museums had far less to spend; in some cases, in fact, they had nothing. Money for purchases usually comes from one of two sources. Either someone gives a museum the cash it needs or the museum uses income from gifts in the past which have been invested. Sometimes donors say that the money they give a museum may be used only to purchase certain kinds of art works. At the Minneapolis Institute of Arts, for example, there is a fund available which can be used only to buy examples of Persian art; in Portland, there is a fund which may be used only for the purchase of English silver. But museum officials tend to discourage such gifts because it limits their freedom. What they prefer and frequently insist on are cash gifts with no strings attached. On the other hand, they may also find something they want to buy for the museum and then try to find a donor who will provide the money they need.

Most museum purchases are made through art dealers clustered in New York along Fifty-seventh Street, and in London, in Paris, and to a lesser extent in Los Angeles. Directors and/or curators of most established museums try to make the rounds of the dealers once a year or at least every other year shopping with the museum's needs and the state of their pocketbooks clearly in mind. In addition, dealers frequently are in contact with the museums to let them know of particular art works which are available or soon will be. Dealers obtain their wares from private individuals, including private collectors and royalty in need of money, from estates, and occasionally from museums themselves. Some dealers are concerned with many kinds of art works. Others specialize. Some such as Knoedler and Company and the Wildenstein Galleries are world-famous. This also was the case with Sir Joseph Duveen, the English supersalesman through whom Andrew Mellon and Samuel Kress acquired many of the paintings they gave to the National Gallery. Although art dealers serve large numbers of private collectors, art museums are among their most valued customers. It was through a dealer, for example, that the Portland Art Museum acquired its Monet water-lily painting. It was through another dealer that this same museum purchased its famous collection of Northwest Indian art in 1948. The collection

had been assembled in the 1920's by an Alaskan school superintendent named Axel Rathmusem. After his death it was sold and
ultimately passed into the hands of the dealer from whom the
museum acquired it. It was through an elite, little-known group of
dealers that the Cleveland Museum of Art spent $5 million in
1965 and 1966 on 150 magnificent works ranging from contemporary paintings to a small gold beaker almost 3,000 years old. The
purchase was one of the largest and most spectacular in the history
of American art museums.[4]

Museums also purchase art works from private collectors. The
world's costliest painting was purchased from such a source in
1967 by the National Gallery of Art in Washington. The painting
is a portrait of a young Italian woman, Ginevra de' Benci, which
Leonardo da Vinci completed in Florence around 1480. The
collector was Prince Franz Josef II of Lichtenstein who received
an estimated $5 million to $6 million for the work, funds it is said
he needed to help govern his country. The Gallery obtained the
money it needed for the purchase from wealthy patrons. The
painting is the only one by da Vinci known to exist outside
Europe.[5] Also from a private collector the Metropolitan Museum
of Art purchased three enormous murals by the Italian master
Tiepolo, the largest being 18 feet high and 11 feet wide. The
murals belonged to a German collector who had brought them to
the United States when he fled his country in the early days of
Hitler's rule. With no place to hang them, he put them into
storage. After his death, his family contacted the Metropolitan and
offered to sell them.[6]

Art Museums also make purchases at auctions. In just four
minutes of bidding in 1961, the Metropolitan acquired the great
Rembrandt painting "Aristotle Contemplating the Bust of
Homer." Its bid was $2,300,000, at that time the highest sum ever

[4] New York *Times*, August 31, 1966.
[5] New York *Times*, February 21, 1967.
[6] New York *Times*, September 20, 1966.

Da Vinci's portrait of Ginevra de'Benci, the world's most costly painting, purchased by the National Gallery of Art from a private collector for more than $5 million. *Courtesy National Gallery of Art*

paid for a painting. When the picture first was displayed so many visitors came to see it they had to wait in line. Although some undoubtedly were attracted by its artistic qualities, many came just to get a look at what was then the world's costliest picture. Even now, years later, there is scarcely a day when someone does not ask for *the* painting. The postcard size "St. George and the Dragon" by the Flemish artist Rogier van der Weyden is another major art work acquired at auction. In November, 1965, the

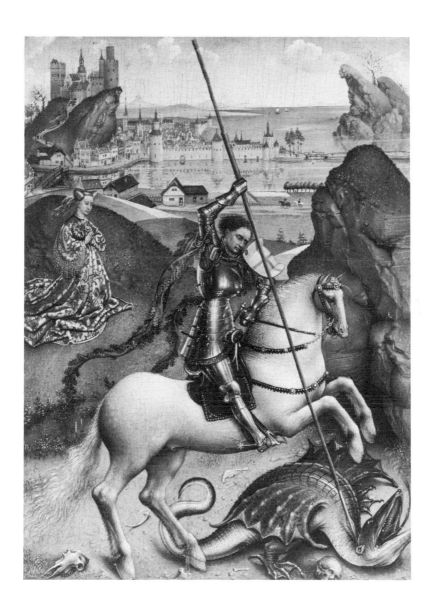

"St. George and the Dragon," which the National Gallery of Art
bought at an auction for $616,000. Actual size of the painting is shown.
Courtesy National Gallery of Art

National Gallery of Art received a letter from a London dealer who reported that the picture, which is but 5 5/8″ high and 4 1/8″ wide, was to be auctioned, although the decision to do so had not been officially announced. Would the National Gallery be interested in bidding? Chief Curator Percy Cott flew to London to inspect the picture, then Gallery Director John Walker flew over. Both were enthusiastic about what they saw. In January the board of trustees set a maximum amount of money that could be offered. Next, a London dealer was hired to bid for the picture in behalf of the Gallery, but he was instructed not to disclose for whom he was bidding. The reasoning was that this might keep the price down. When a major museum shows itself to be interested in a work, its interest sometimes attracts other bidders which in turn may drive the price up. In the end, several bidders were involved. They included the Metropolitan Museum, which was the third from the last to drop out, and a Czechoslovakian count, an expert in Flemish paintings, who was the last to give in. For $616,000—or $26,552 per square inch—the painting became the National Gallery's.[7] Often, of course, the circumstances of a purchase are less glamorous. At least two highly popular exhibits at art museums come from department stores. The fourteen heraldic banners of the Knights of the Garter displayed with the armor collection at the Metropolitan Museum of Art are copies obtained in a sale at Wannamaker's, the Philadelphia department store. The two fifteenth century stone camels that guard the entrance to the Seattle Art Museum, and originally guarded the tomb of a Chinese emperor, came to the museum at a very good price from Gump's in San Francisco.

---

[7] When the Gallery first became interested in the "St. George" its staff was not at all sure that it was the work of the artist credited with having painted it, Jan Van Eyck. But it was so fine a painting, it was decided to try for it anyway. After its acquisition, research based on a comparison of painting styles showed it to be the work of Rogier van der Weyden, a student of Van Eyck's.

One of the two 15th century camels by a Chinese sculptor which the Seattle Art Museum purchased from a San Francisco department store. *Courtesy Seattle Art Museum*

The heraldic banners displayed with the armor at the Metropolitan Museum of Art also were department store purchases. *Courtesy Metropolitan Museum of Art: Photograph, Gary Winograd*

THE POSSIBILITY OF ERROR

When museum officials are making up their minds about buying a work of art or accepting a gift, they want to know with certainty who the artist is and when the work was done. One reason, of course, is their concern with historical accuracy. Another is their concern with the value of the work involved. As was the case with the National Gallery's "St. George and the Dragon," it sometimes is very difficult to tell who the artist was. With a painting, the artist's signature may be a guide, but not always. Sometimes there is no signature. Forgery also is a problem. As long as man has created art, there have been clever craftsmen who have imitated the work of the best artists and tried to sell it as genuine at prices such artists command. Just a short time before this was written, the artist Marc Chagall had an opportunity to examine one of "his" works only to discover it wasn't his at all. It is said that in the United States alone, there are more paintings that carry the signature of the famous artist Jean Corot than Corot painted. The artists Utrillo, Maillol, and Van Gogh also are highly popular with forgers. There are so many fake Van Gogh's, in fact, that those known to exist are described in a catalog. In evaluating a work for possible purchase, a curator will examine it carefully, perhaps compare it with others by the same artist, perhaps get an opinion from one or two other experts, review its history of ownership, and make his judgment. At times, his judgment is that the work is of high quality, but the artist is hard to pin down. Then the curator may engage in a good deal of research, comparing the styles of various painters or, as was the case with "St. George and the Dragon," the museum may go ahead and buy the work and do the research later. However, there are situations when, even after a great deal of effort, the answers are not forthcoming. For example, the art museum at Fenimore House in Cooperstown, New York, owns a handsome unsigned painting of a well-dressed Negro boy which appears to date to the early years of the nineteenth century. But its curators have been unable to identify the artist, the style of painting, or the boy. Now they play a waiting game. They keep their eyes and their ears open for possible clues, and they have asked other experts elsewhere to do the same. Years may elapse before such a puzzle is solved, if it ever is.

In evaluating a work a curator may turn to science for help. Examination under ultraviolet and infrared light, for example, will indicate whether the surface has been repainted, repaired, or otherwise changed. When a painting from a Paris dealer arrived at the Seattle Art Museum, everything looked fine. But ultraviolet examination showed that the picture had had a face lifting. Most of the original painting was missing; in its place was the work of a modern-day restorer. X ray also is used. Boston's Museum of the Fine Arts was considering a painting said to be by Joseph Turner, the English landscape artist. However, an X ray found another painting underneath whose style showed it had been painted well after Turner died. The painting on the surface obviously was a forgery.

The research laboratory at the Museum of Fine Arts, one of the most advanced installations of its kind, also uses a variety of other techniques to determine how old an object is and where it comes from. For example, a spectroscope provides an analysis, or a kind of fingerprint, of the chemical elements in a sample of paint, fabric, metal, or clay which then can be matched against a file of existing "fingerprints" whose age and origin already are known. If a paint pigment is involved, the museum's researchers can turn to a collection of thousands of pigments from all over the world, from 3,000 B.C. onward. Prussian blue, for example, originated during the eighteenth century. If a researcher finds this pigment used in a work said to be by a seventeenth century painter, then obviously something is amiss. In recent years, the museum's laboratory also has been using microbeam analysis and the laser beam in determining what art works are made of. In microbeam analysis a hypodermic needle the size of a human hair is inserted into a painting. When it is withdrawn it carries with it a minute core containing samples of all the layers of paint and varnish used. The core is bombarded with electrons. These generate measurable X

A scalpel is used to uncover the original paint on a 14th century Pietà in the research laboratory at Boston's Museum of Fine Arts. *Courtesy Museum of Fine Arts, Boston*

rays which in turn provide a complete chemical analysis of the painting from varnish through to the backing. The laser is used for analysis of many kinds of materials. Its beam turns an almost invisible sample to vapor which then is chemically analyzed.

Sometimes many methods are used together in learning about an object. A handsome Greek vase that came to the Boston laboratory for examination was said to be 2,500 years old. It seemed in excellent condition. No cracks were visible, the paint was sound, and the painted designs were well formed. Examination under ultraviolet light revealed that the designs had been repainted. Further examination by infrared light and by X ray showed that at one time the vase had been badly cracked and had been repaired and repainted. From the spectroscope and a Geiger counter it was learned that modern paint and varnish covered the surface, not the ancient glaze of iron oxide that should have been there.

Not too many years ago a skillful forger could get away with a great deal more than he can today. One of the most successful was a Dutch artist named Han van Meegeren. As Russell Lynes tells the story in his book *The Tastemakers*,[8] van Meegeren took to forging as a means of revenge for the lack of recognition he had received for his own paintings. The man whose work he decided to copy was Johannes Vermeer, the famous seventeenth century Dutch painter, whose paintings command prices of a half million dollars and more. To prepare himself, he spent four years experimenting with Vermeer's techniques and also developed paints that produced the same effect Vermeer's did. Then he painted his first "Vermeer" which he called "Christ at Emmaus," had it touched up to look like an old painting, and offered it through a dealer as a forgotten masterpiece. It was sold for $378,000 to the Boymans Museum in Rotterdam. Experts described it as "one of the greatest Vermeers in existence." Van Meegeren then proceeded to paint five more "Vermeers," bringing prices that ranged from $264,000 to $750,000. The last one he painted was bought by Nazi Field Marshal Hermann Goering after the Germans had occupied the Netherlands during World War II. It was this sale that proved to be van Meegeren's undoing. After the war he was arrested for having collaborated with the Nazis by selling Goering such an important painting. In his defense, he confessed that the work was

[8] Russell Lynes, *The Tastemakers*, New York: Harper, 1954, p. 278 ff.

a forgery, and, in fact, had fooled the Nazi. No one believed him until in the courtroom he painted still another "Vermeer." In the end, he was sentenced to a year in prison for forging Vermeer's signature, but soon after he died of a heart attack.

Although none of van Meegeren's efforts reached American museums, those of another master did. He was an Italian stone-cutter named Alceo Dossena who in the 1920's turned out hundreds of pieces of sculpture in the styles of Roman, Greek, Medieval, and Renaissance artists. To give his creations the appearance of great age, he resorted to various techniques: he broke them; he buried them in compost; he dipped them in acid. When they were ready, he turned them over to a pair of dishonest dealers who conjured up stories as to where they came from and sold them. Some of his work found its way into such treasure houses as the Metropolitan Museum and the Frick Collection in New York, the Cleveland Museum of Art, and Boston's Museum of Fine Arts. Lynes reports that in the United States alone $1.5 million was spent on Dossena's sculptures before they were spotted as fakes.

WHAT TO BUY

Decisions on what to add to a museum's collections are not always easy to make. The quality of a work and its authenticity are of extreme importance. So is its value in illustrating some aspect of art history. If a purchase is involved, the price being asked must be considered. However, such decisions are even more difficult in museums concerned with the work of contemporary artists, for they must reach conclusions about new approaches and techniques that often are not yet clearly understood or even classified in any way. Alfred H. Barr, Jr., director of museum collections at New York's Museum of Modern Art, once explained his museum's approach in this way: "The museum is aware that it often may guess wrong in its acquisitions. When it acquires a dozen recent paintings, it will be lucky if in ten years three still will seem worth looking at, if in twenty years only one should survive. For the future, the important problem is to acquire this one: the other nine will be forgiven—and forgotten. But meanwhile we live in the present and for the present these other nine will seem just as necessary and useful. . . . Sooner or later, time will eliminate them."

On the other hand, in focusing on established artists, the National Gallery of Art in Washington has quite a different approach. It does not accept a work for its permanent collections unless the artist has been dead at least twenty years. In all cases, however, a museum's director and curators recommend what to buy and what to accept, but the final decision rests with the board of trustees. In some museums, an acquisitions committee of trustees has responsibility and the board accepts its decisions; in others the entire board participates. More often than not a director's recommendations are accepted. However, a lack of money or disagreement with the wisdom of the recommendation can stand in the way.

GIFTS FROM THE GROUND

Over the years excavations at the sites of early civilizations, such as those in Egypt, Greece, and Rome, have been yet another source of art treasures. In fact, the first director of the Metropolitan Museum, Louis Palma di Cesnola, was appointed after he sold it a large group of ancient objects such as glassware, bronzes, vases, and jewelry which he obtained from tombs in Cyprus.[9] The imposing collections of Egyptian art at the Museum of Fine Arts in Boston and at the Metropolitan Museum are largely the result of permanent expeditions the museums maintained in Egypt from just after the turn of the century to the start of World War II. However, the great increase in the cost of such undertakings and the growing restrictions by foreign governments on removing art treasures today have ruled out this approach for most museums. Instead they rely on gifts and the offerings of dealers.

The major American archaeological expeditions still at work

[9] Di Cesnola was an Italian nobleman who came to the United States during the Civil War to help train Union troops. As his reward, President Lincoln named him U.S. Consul to Cyprus. In his free time, he excavated.

are sent out by universities. The two leaders in this activity are the Oriental Institute of the University of Chicago and the University Museum at the University of Pennsylvania in Philadelphia. As the earlier Egyptian expeditions, their primary objective is increasing the knowledge of man's development and behavior. But another objective certainly is the accumulation of art objects for display and for research. The University Museum in Philadelphia serves both as a museum of art and a training center for archaeologists. At present it has some twenty expeditions at work in such places as Jordan, where a town dating from the eighth century B.C. has been uncovered; in southern Italy, where a search is underway for the lost city of Sybarius; in Turkey, where ancient settlements are being excavated at Gordian; and in Guatemala at the ancient religious city of Tikal. Some projects require a team of but three or four professors and students and perhaps two or three seasons of work. Others, such as the extensive excavations at Gordian and at Tikal, have involved dozens of scholars and years of effort. At best, however, an expedition will share its finds with the country involved on a 50–50 basis. In several countries, increasingly concerned with their heritage, nothing may be taken out. For a number of years this has been the case in Egypt. It represents a drastic change from the days of the big museum expeditions.

In that period Boston's Museum of Fine Arts alone excavated some twenty sites up and down the length of the Nile from Giza near Cairo, south to the Sudan and the Land of the Kush. One of the most fascinating of its finds was the hidden tomb and the remarkable gold funeral furniture of Queen Hetep-Heres, mother of the Pharaoh Cheops, at Giza in 1925.[10] The entrance to the tomb was discovered by the expedition's photographer while he was taking pictures in the ancient royal cemetery. One of the legs

[10] The men responsible were the late Dr. George A. Reisner and Dows Dunham, who today is the museum's curator emeritus of Egyptian Art. The account included here is drawn from conversations with Mr. Dunham and from his *The Egyptian Department and Its Excavations* published by the museum.

of his tripod sunk in a soft spot. The soft spot turned out to be part of an elongated patch of plaster. The plaster covered a trench filled with blocks of limestone that sealed a stairway to a tunnel that led to a stone-filled shaft one hundred feet deep. At the base of the shaft was a block of stone set in a wall beyond which was a burial chamber. But months were needed to empty the shaft. What puzzled archaeologists as they worked toward the bottom was that this tomb did not have a structure built over it as others did. What excited them was that obviously it had not been opened since it first was sealed. When finally the block of stone that led to the burial chamber had been removed, flashlight beams revealed a room about 15 feet long, 8 feet wide, and 6 feet high. Much of the nearest wall was filled with a stone sarcophagus. Atop this coffin was a pile of gold tubes. On the floor were stone vases, a pile of pottery, a copper jug and a copper basin, the leg of a golden lion which apparently had been part of a piece of furniture, and many bars, sheets, and thin strips of gold.

What was even more curious was the arrangement of the room. Usually the coffin was placed in the funeral chamber first against a

A painting of the tomb chamber of Queen Hetep-Heres I, made when it was first opened. *Courtesy Museum of Fine Arts, Boston*

far wall; then during the funeral the corpse was placed in the coffin and it was closed. Next, the furniture and other personal articles Egyptians believed would be needed in the afterworld were brought in, then finally the cooking equipment and containers of food that also would be needed. In this case, the pottery had been placed in the room first, then apparently the furniture, and finally the coffin. It soon became clear that the gold bars, sheets, and strips were all that remained of the furniture, that the wood that had supported the gold had decayed to dust and that the gold lay just where it had fallen. If the room was to be understood, and if the furniture was to be reconstructed, each object and each fragment would have to be recorded in terms of its position and its relationship to the other pieces. What made the task even more difficult was that no funeral furniture from this period had been found before and nothing was known of how it had looked originally. In addition, the room was so cluttered one could not enter without disturbing the contents. Moreover, in this tomb situated a hundred feet below ground there was no light and no ventilation, and it was uncomfortably hot.

Yet the task was undertaken and after almost two years of painstaking effort the room was cleared and its contents recorded. Once lights and fans had been moved in, the archaeologists set to work. As a first step, they arbitrarily divided the room into one-foot squares. Then a full-size plan was made of each square, with everything that could be seen, down to the smallest sliver, drawn exactly where it lay. Then a photograph was made of the square. Finally, each object from the square was carefully removed and numbered, with the number recorded in its appropriate position on the plan. When everything that could be seen in a square had been completely cleared, the archaeologists moved on to another.[11]

---

[11] One of the pieces they removed carried an inscription in hieroglyphics which identified the owner of the tomb. It read: "Mother of the King of Upper and Lower Egypt, Follower of Horus, Guide to the Ruler, Favorite one, she whose every word is done for her, the daughter of the God's body, Hetep-Heres." Or, the mother of the great pharaoh Cheops.

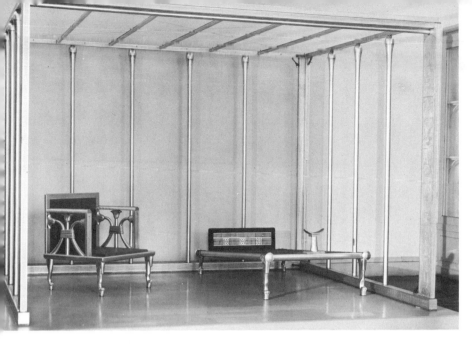

A reconstruction of Hetep-Heres' armchair, bed, and bed canopy intended for her use in afterlife, based on remains found in the queen's tomb chamber. The curved object at the high end of the bed is a headrest; a footboard is at the lower end. *Courtesy Museum of Fine Arts, Boston*

As space became available in the room they moved in wooden boxes to sit on, then a mattress so that they could work in greater comfort. Eventually the room was emptied, but 1,500 pages of notes and drawings and 1,700 photographs detailed what it had been like. Based on this record, the furniture was reconstructed. It consisted of a carrying chair, a headrest sheathed in gold and silver sheets, an armchair, a bed with gold-sheathed legs like those of a lion, and a collapsible bed canopy, part of which were the gold tubes found on top of the coffin. The reconstructed furniture is in the government museum in Cairo. However, a copy of what was rebuilt is displayed in the Egyptian galleries in Boston.

But what of the sarcophagus? When the room finally was emptied the time had come to open it. When the heavy stone lid at last was raised, however, nothing was inside. The archaeologists then turned to a section of the wall that had been plastered over. Behind the plaster, in the Egyptian custom, was a chest containing the queen's internal organs which had been embalmed and wrapped in four packets. But the mystery remained. Where was the mummy? After much study, the archaeologists concluded that Cheops had first had his mother buried elsewhere near the tomb of her husband; that soon after she was buried, tomb robbers unwrapped her mummy, stripped it of its jewelry, then left the body to be dragged off and devoured by jackals. It is not clear whether Cheops ever learned that his mother's mummy had been destroyed, although the archaeologists did not think it likely. If he had known, they reasoned, there would not have been a second burial, for it would have been pointless without the mummy. Instead, they speculated, he may have been convinced by those who did know and wished to escape his wrath that the mummy should be moved to a new tomb closer to where his would stand so that all members of his family might be with him in afterlife. Through such a maneuver, he never would have learned of the dreadful deed. In any case, the empty coffin, the embalmed organs, and the furnishings of the plundered tomb were moved to their new location, then sealed. Whoever made the arrangements appears to have been completely successful. Almost five thousand years passed before the secret of the missing mummy came to light.

ACCESSIONING

When a work is acquired by an art museum, its first stop after it arrives at the shipping room is the registrar's office where it is "accessioned", or officially made a part of the museum's collections. Ordinarily this involves a number of steps. Its pedigree is recorded —its title, what it is and where it was acquired, its size and condition, its age, name of the artist, his birth date, and if he is dead, when he died, the artistic school or group with which he is identified, and often any history of the work available. To further identify it the work is photographed and given an accessions number. The number ordinarily is shown on the label that accompanies it when it is displayed. The first number usually indicates the year in which the object was obtained and the next the order in which it was received that year. If the accession consisted of a gift or purchase of several works rather than one, then a third number may be assigned for each item in a group. For example, if a painting bears the number 67.28.4, it means that it was acquired in 1967, that it was the twenty-eighth acquisition that year, and that it was one of four or more pieces acquired together through a single purchase, gift, or bequest. The registrar at the National Gallery of Art in Washington, D.C., has three registration cards for each work. One is filed by title, another by the artist's name, and the third by the object's location. This third card is particularly useful to the registrar in that one of his responsibilities is to know at any given moment where each of the museum's possessions is. This is a challenging assignment when one considers that thousands of objects are involved, that many may be spread over acres of floorspace and that others may be on loan to institutions all over the country or the world. Still another of the registrar's responsibilities is maintaining a precise inventory of what the museum has in the way of art works. The day I visited the National Gallery, for example, the registrar's inventory, including objects in the museum on loan and for special purposes, was as follows:

Paintings	2,262
Sculptures	1,733
Prints, drawings	25,206
Decorative objects, including vases, rugs, tapestries	442
Photographs	1,442

The total came to 32,597 objects. Of course, some museums have many more possessions and others have far fewer. At the Museum of Fine Arts in Boston, when one asks, he is told the museum has as many objects as the number of pebbles on Crane's Beach in Ipswich, Massachusetts, plus one. However, the number of objects a museum possesses is in itself meaningless. What is of importance is the quality of what it has and the completeness of its collections.

EXHIBITS

Not too many years ago, the emphasis in art museums was on showing as much as possible, on crowding cases and walls with all they could hold. Today the emphasis is on displaying far less so that each work is shown to its best advantage and may generate a response on its own. Ideally this means displaying a work so handsomely and so cleverly that the surroundings drop away and all that remains for the viewer is the work itself. In practical terms this may be difficult for a museum to achieve, but some do very well.

It is the curator who has responsibility for displaying a work of art. In smaller museums he may plan a gallery and hang the pictures himself, or, if there is no curator, the director does so. In larger museums several persons may be involved in planning and installing a gallery. Often paintings are arranged by historical period, school, and artist, but once the groupings have been established, there remains the problem of which pictures should be displayed together. What is involved is something like working out a puzzle. Color, size, subject matter, and style all must be taken into account since the appearance of each picture is affected by the characteristics of its neighbors. Sometimes pictures are equally spaced down to the last tenth of an inch. In other cases, they may be grouped in two's and three's. Whatever the approach, when pictures are at home with one another they all benefit; when they are not, they all suffer.

The height at which a picture is hung also is of importance. Usually the center is at eye level for the average adult, or 58 to 60 inches from the floor. But this, too, depends on the needs of the pictures and the gallery. Another consideration is lighting. Museums blessed with extensive skylighting rely heavily on natural light, supplemented by small spotlights. When the National Gallery in Washington is open at night, it tries to approximate daylight through the use of large floodlights, much as baseball parks do. The gallery's floods are in the attic and shine through skylights. Many lighting approaches are used, however. One of the

Changes in methods of display over the years at the Metropolitan Museum of Art. Top: American Sculpture Gallery, 1907. Bottom: Chinese Sculpture Gallery, 1967. *Courtesy Metropolitan Museum of Art: bottom photograph, Gary Winograd*

The skylighting and floodlights used to reproduce daylight in the galleries of the National Gallery of Art. *Courtesy National Gallery of Art*

Paintings hung in semi-darkness at the Virginia Museum of Fine Arts. *Courtesy Virginia Museum of Fine Arts*

most effective is in use at the Virginia Museum of Fine Arts in Richmond. There paintings are hung in darkened galleries with soft lighting focused only on the pictures.

Hanging an exhibit of paintings may take days or weeks, depending on the task. At the National Gallery the curators first work with blueprints of the walls to be used. On these they position photographs of the paintings which have been printed to scale. Once a first draft has been completed, the works themselves are placed on the floor against a wall in the positions selected for them. To protect their frames, they are set on rubber kneeling pads. If changes are necessary, and often they are, the paintings are moved from position to position until the curators feel comfortable with the arrangement and the overall appearance of the room. Stacked haphazardly on the floor before they are hung, priceless masterpieces may look as if they came from a run-down pawnshop. When they have been arranged as they should be, as one curator commented, "They sing."

Where sculpture and other three-dimensional works are involved, the problems are somewhat different. For one thing, these objects should be seen from all sides. Moreover, they often must rest on pedestals or other specially constructed mounts. In preparing a gallery of sculpture, a large museum often turns to a designer for advice, either someone from its own staff or a consultant it hires. At the Metropolitan Museum of Art a curator in charge of such an exhibit will select the important works to be featured and also decide which pieces should be grouped. Then the designer, working closely with the curator, plans the setting, the arrangement, the mounts, the color of the room, the lighting, and other details. The objective never varies. It is to eliminate all distractions so that for the visitor there is only the object.

Borrowing and Lending. Those museums "without" borrow from those "with" either on a long-term basis to strengthen their collections or on a short-term basis for special exhibits. What makes such exchanges possible is that most large museums and a number of smaller ones have more high-quality material than they need for their research or could hope to display. Rather than keep unused objects of great beauty in a vault where they do no one any good, they lend them so that they can be enjoyed elsewhere. The Metropolitan Museum has twenty thousand such works on long-term loan to other museums and also to government offices, hospitals, libraries, and schools. One of its many borrowers is the Roberson Memorial Center in Binghamton, New York, where some two hundred works form an exhibit which otherwise might never have been seen in that area. The Portland Art Museum in Oregon is a smaller institution that lends its treasures. In a recent year over a hundred objects were out on loan for several months at a time to such institutions as the Boise, Idaho, Gallery of Art and the Vancouver, Canada, Art Gallery.

When special exhibits are being assembled, museums often part with the very best they have for short periods. It was this way that the Toledo Museum of Art in Ohio, the California Palace of the Legion of Honor in San Francisco, and Boston's Museum of Fine Arts put together a spectacular show for their cities on the men who painted during "The Age of Rembrandt." After pooling the works they owned, they borrowed priceless paintings from forty-nine other museums and a number of private collectors throughout Europe and North America. A total of 107 works were brought together, with the three museums sharing the cost. Then the paintings were shown in each of the museums involved and finally returned to their owners. Although few cooperative shows are of such quality, each year many are organized along these lines.

EDUCATION

Through tours, lectures, films, art lessons and art courses, publications, junior museum programs, TV and radio shows, and traveling exhibits, art museums work very hard to increase the public's understanding of art, elevate taste, and, not incidentally, expand their audiences. It is safe to say that millions of adults and children are exposed to such efforts each year, voluntarily or otherwise.

At the Philadelphia Museum of Art, there is a paid education staff of forty full-time and part-time specialists. At the Art Institute of Chicago, twenty-one staff members are involved, along with more than a hundred trained volunteer teachers. In fact, every established art museum has at least one person, and generally more, whose job is "education." As at the Art Institute of Chicago, many museums also have volunteer teachers, or docents as they are known, to take school groups on tours through the museum. Often such volunteers are members of the local Junior League or the local chapter of the American Association of University Women. Usually they have a background in art history; however, frequently a museum also provides some training. One of the most elaborate such programs is carried out at Chicago's Art Institute. Women interested in volunteering attend school a full day a week for eight weeks and also have homework assignments. Finally, they take an examination. Those who pass then prepare an outline for a lecture they would give visiting classes. If this is approved, they give the lecture to three different groups. The third time it is tape-recorded and the tape recording is then reviewed. Needless to say, not everyone makes the grade.

A visiting class and its museum teacher. *Courtesy Philadelphia Museum of Art: photograph, Joseph Nettis*

Most youngsters who live anywhere near an art museum have participated in one or more class visits to the museum by the time they are in high school. Often such visits are tied in with what they have been studying, such as the Age of Exploration or life in Colonial times. In other cases, they are aimed at giving the children a sense of the pleasure and fascination to be found in art works.

In the largest museums, upward of 100,000 school children a year visit with their classes. Typically, teachers are sent material in advance so that their classes may have some idea of what to expect. When the pupils arrive, a docent meets them and off they go. At the National Gallery of Art a class generally will see five or six pictures and a piece of sculpture. At each stop, the youngsters sit on the floor, listen to a brief explanation of the work they are looking at, then ask any questions they have. In some of the larger museums there is a children's room or a junior museum where the visit begins. At the Art Institute of Chicago, the junior museum includes a permanent display on the uses of light in art; a temporary display on one other aspect of art such as color, motion, or size; a changing exhibit of paintings, prints, or sculpture; a children's art library; and a children's museum shop. Once a class has been shown the junior museum, it then visits one or two of the main galleries. Some museum visits involve doing as well as looking. At the Cranbrook Gallery of Art, north of Detroit, visiting classes are given art lessons as well as a tour. As part of a lesson on portraits at Boston's Museum of Fine Arts, youngsters first see a film on the subject, then visit the galleries for a guided look at portraits, then return to the children's room to create portraits of their own.

Although there is great enthusiasm in the museums for programs such as these, there also are problems. One such problem is that many school teachers know little of art and how to make use of an art museum in their classroom work. In line with this, the U. S. Office of Education and the National Gallery have organized a six-week training program for school teachers which covers the history of art and the use of art museums in education. The first summer of the program, forty teachers from all over the United States were brought to Washington to participate.

Another problem that ought to concern more museum people is the noise and crowding in the galleries as children are brought through, which often makes it difficult for the children and other visitors to use a museum properly. On a weekday morning at the National Gallery, for example, with children, teachers, and docents coming and going at a great rate, the place resembles an airlines terminal. As one solution, a few museums do not open their doors to the public until noon, reserving morning hours for visiting classes, but other museums cannot, or will not, do this. Meanwhile, as the number of school children brought to museums increases and the number of adult visitors grows, maintaining a pleasant atmosphere for everyone becomes more and more difficult.

For youngsters interested enough to come to a museum on their own, many museums also offer programs on Saturdays and during summer months. The Toledo Museum of Art offers a five-year program in art appreciation and art history. The William Rockhill Nelson Gallery in Kansas City, Missouri, has creative art

Saturday art classes at Toledo Museum of Art. *Courtesy Toledo Museum of Art: photograph, Herral Long*

workshops for children as young as four and five. The City Art Museum in St. Louis sponsors lectures for high school students on such subjects as Modern Painting and Aspects of Ancient Art. The Brooklyn Museum in New York offers workshops in making masks, toys, mosaics, and puppets, as well as educational treasure hunts[12] and a chance for older children to learn about the museum by working as volunteers in the libraries and the gift shop. Some museums also offer college-level courses for credit. For example, the Toledo Museum of Art serves in a sense as an art department for the University of Toledo, just as the Portland Art Museum in Oregon does for Reed College. Others, including Minneapolis, Chicago, and Boston, also maintain professional schools for artists.

For school classes and others who are unable to visit a museum, there are "extension" programs through which exhibits are sent traveling. In New York City each month the Museum of Modern Art sends exhibits on art plus lending libraries of books and art reproductions to sixty high schools. From the Seattle Art Museum "Treasure Boxes" of art objects regularly go out to classrooms in the city's schools.

From the Virginia Museum of Fine Arts in Richmond four Artmobiles travel to schools, colleges, and towns all over the state carrying Chinese and Egyptian art, landscape paintings, portraits, sculpture—anything, in fact, one would find at the museum itself. When they arrive in a town, they remain as long as a week so that everyone can visit. The newest and largest of these traveling art galleries is 57 feet long and 10 feet wide. To protect the art work it carries, it is air conditioned, humidified, and as burglarproof and jounceproof as can be. The most massive extension program in the United States is run by the Federal government through the National Gallery. Films, filmstrips, exhibits of framed art repro-

---

[12] Clue 2-4A: "A brave man is represented in the SCULPTURE COURT. He is called a _____, much admired and respected for some great deed which he performed. The sculpture is not meant to be a _____ of any particular man. Its purpose is to convey some of the qualities that a heroic person might have. . . ."

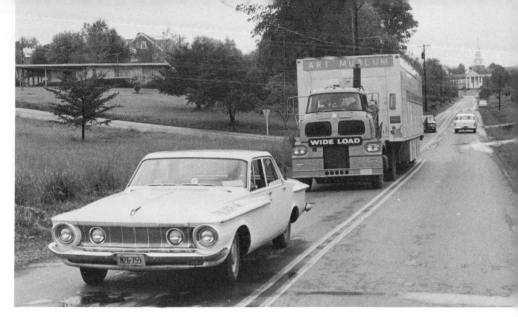

An artmobile operated by the Virginia Museum of Fine Arts. *Courtesy Virginia Museum of Fine Arts*

ductions, and slide lectures with recorded talks on more than a dozen subjects are in continuous use by schools, colleges, and private groups throughout the country.

Of course, many museum programs are primarily for adults. When the Philadelphia Museum of Art had a major exhibit of the paintings of Edouard Manet, for example, there were free illustrated lectures, daily gallery talks, tape-recorded tours for rent, and a major symposium at which scholars presented papers on the painter. Some museums have elaborate schedules of lectures, courses, and tours for adults. In Detroit and Minneapolis the museums even have "fine arts luncheons" for businessmen at which aspects of the arts are explained. Here, of course, financial support is an objective, along with education.

Television and radio also are widely used by art museums. In fact, the Museum of Fine Arts in Boston is completely wired for TV, with special outlets in every gallery. Some art museums sponsor trips so that treasures elsewhere may be viewed firsthand. The Philadelphia Museum of Art has sponsored trips to Charleston, Newport, Rhode Island, and Washington and Baltimore for

A television show filmed at the Museum of Fine Arts, Boston. *Courtesy Museum of Fine Arts, Boston*

this purpose. It also takes art lovers abroad. In 1967 the museum sponsored a one-month guided trip to the Orient at $2,500 per person for those interested in Oriental art. Boston's Museum of Fine Arts is another that is in the travel business. In recent years it has sponsored guided tours of art treasures in Egypt and Russia.

The Metropolitan Museum is the only museum to date that offers a series of "Seminars in Art." These are published and sold by the Book-of-the-Month Club. Full-page advertisements ask: "Are you one of the many who admire Mona Lisa for the wrong reasons?" If you are, and this worries you, the seminars will help you overcome your ignorance.

RESEARCH

Two important aspects of museum research already have been discussed: identifying the artist who created an art work and determining whether a work is authentic. But museum research goes well beyond these objectives. Its broad concerns are learning more about art, artists, and the significance of both in history. As a result, one of the major responsibilities of every art museum is the development of detailed scholarly catalogs on the objects in each of its important collections. A good catalog will provide a complete life history of each of the works involved, covering its artist, importance, condition, school and period, age, origin, previous owners, where it has been displayed, and books and articles about it. The result is a permanent reference to which historians and others can turn for accurate, complete information. Unfortunately there are few such catalogs on the collections in American art museums. One of the problems is cost. As much as $30,000 may be involved in the preparation of a single volume. Another is time. Months and months of effort may be required, and most curators have too much else to do to make the time available. Even when funds do exist, it is often necessary to bring in an outside scholar to do the job.

This lack of historical material on what they own is a major weakness of art museums in the United States and a basis for criticism by museum people here and abroad. Speaking in Cleveland at the fiftieth anniversary celebration of the Cleveland Museum of Art, Sir Frank Francis, director of the British Museum, warned against allowing educational activities, publicity, and the interests of the "ordinary man in the street" to reduce the time the museum scholar has for research. To help meet the problem, the Ford Foundation has been providing art museums with funds to prepare catalogs. To date, over $400,000 has gone to twenty-four museums to help them in the preparation of thirty-six such works. The grant is a generous one, but there is so much to be done that it represents only a beginning.

Museum scholarship can take many forms. One of the curators of arms and armor I talked with at the Metropolitan Museum was leaving for Italy the following week to examine lists of armor compiled in the early seventeenth century which might yield clues to the identity of some of the museum's holdings. At about the same time, some 250 art scholars were assembling at the De Young Museum in San Francisco to examine and discuss the museum's great collection of Oriental art. The day I spent at the Museum of Fine Arts in Boston, an Oxford University professor who is an expert on the art of Mesopotamia also was a visitor. He had come to compare two sets of ancient ivory carvings the museum owns—

one from Mesopotamia, the other from the Sudan—to determine in what ways, if any, they were related. Some weeks before I called at the Portland Art Museum, a professor from the University of California had been there. His objective was to examine the museum's Greek vases for a catalog of vases he was developing. All over the country, and all over the world, the process goes on. Often the scholar is gathering information for a particular project. At other times he studies the art works in a collection to improve his knowledge of their characteristics and relationships. Of course photographs and color transparencies of the major collections often are available for his use. What brings him to see the originals is that they are original. One may learn a great deal from a transparency, but he cannot know all there is to know about an object until he has it there in front of him and if possible holds it in his hands.

CONSERVATION

Art museums engage in a continuing struggle to protect their irreplaceable treasures against the ravages of old age and modern times. Aging is a problem unto itself. Scientists are not yet fully certain just why after a hundred years in a museum a textile suddenly will break down and turn to powder or why an old painting that appears sound enough abruptly will twist and blister while others the same age do not. It seems clear that light and humidity play their parts, but just how is a question that still is unanswered.

Along with these uncertainties are the realities of life today—the problems that derive from increasing numbers of people in a museum and the effects of dirt and air pollution. What complicates matters still further are the many different kinds of materials to be cared for. They include paint, canvas, wood, metal, paper, cloth, stone, clay, and glass, each with its own requirements. Moreover, modern artists sometimes employ materials that have not been widely used in art works before—enamel paint is one example—and that may require new techniques and approaches.

A museum conducts its defense against decay on two fronts. On one hand, it restores, repairs, and cleans its art works. On the other, it tries to control the environment so that conditions in its gallery will not have a negative effect. How well a museum can meet these responsibilities depends largely on the money it has available to do the job. Many museums do very well; some do not.

One of the continuing tasks of restoration is cleaning and revarnishing paintings. Older varnishes turn yellow and change the colors of the painting. What was intended as blue sky, for example, may now appear gray-green. Once the yellow film has

John Finlayson of Boston's Museum of Fine Arts cleans "The Head of Cyrus Brought to Queen Tomyris," a painting by Peter Paul Rubens. *Courtesy Museum of Fine Arts, Boston*

been removed and is replaced with a modern nonyellowing varnish, a picture can be seen as the artist saw it. Another task is repairing the cracks and blisters paintings may acquire. Frequently repainting is also necessary. In the past the approach was to make repainting look as much like the original work as possible. Now the restorer fills in the affected area with a color that closely matches the original paint, but he does not try to make his work look like the work of the artist. The result is that from a distance a picture looks complete. On close examination, however, one will be able to find just where restoration has been done. At times the canvas that supports a painting will deteriorate. It then must be removed from the paint and replaced in a process known as relining. This is a tricky, time-consuming business, particularly when the paint is fragile and thin.

Another of the conservator's tasks is repairing torn prints and manuscripts. It is his job to mesh the torn fibers of the paper so expertly that it is almost impossible to spot the damage. Occasionally special problems arise with paper. A famous artist may have sketched on both sides of a sheet and the paper must be split so that the two drawings can be hung separately. Or it may be that total restoration of a print is necessary. This was the case with a fifteenth century Flemish woodcut "Christ on the Cross" at the Museum of Fine Arts in Boston. The print was dirty and brittle and had been partially destroyed by silverfish and woodworms. The first task was to remove its tattered remains from the wood panel that supported it. First the print was moistened, then painstakingly removed piece by piece. Finally, each piece was carefully cleaned and remounted on handmade paper that matched the original 500-year-old paper both in color and texture. The print is shown, before and after restoration, on page 93.

A conservator at the De Young Museum in San Francisco devotes full time to caring for the museum's collection of Oriental Art. When we talked, he was working on a giant fifteenth century Japanese Buddha (page 94). Worms had eaten away large portions of the inside of the statue, along with some of the surface. In

"Christ on the Cross," a 15th
century Flemish woodcut,
before and after restoration.
*Courtesy Museum of Fine
Arts, Boston*

A worm-eaten 13th century Japanese Buddha after restoration at the M. H. De Young Memorial Museum in San Francisco. *Courtesy De Young Museum: Avery Brundage Collection*

addition, the Buddha's lacquer had dried out and was peeling. To strengthen the statue and prevent further decay, the conservator gave it hypodermic injections of a special plastic. To restore the lacquer, he first heated and softened the remaining pieces, then glued them back in place.

When I visited one of the two conservation departments at the Metropolitan Museum in New York, one of the conservators was putting together a Roman glass bowl that had been obtained in

117 fragments. It was a slow and tedious job, but exciting to observe as the bowl regained its lost identity.

Controlling the environment for a work of art is another important aspect of conservation. As we have seen, a continuing problem is controlling the "touchers," those people who thoughtlessly handle fragile works and in the process expose them to the danger of damage. The lint, dust, and grime people bring into the museum is another problem. Dirt has a bad effect on all art works, but it is the old tapestries that usually suffer most since they are too fragile to be dusted or vacuumed. Indeed, so careful are the museums with them that they may be cleaned only once every ten years. As might be expected, the problem of dirt is the most serious in the biggest and busiest cities. To deal with conditions in New York, the Metropolitan Museum not only has a force of one hundred sweepers and cleaners, it is installing an air door which will suck superficial dirt off visitors as they enter.

Museums must also contend with the effect of invisible commercial and industrial gases that seep into the galleries from outside. In at least one museum ancient bronzes coated with a lovely green patina have been turned the color of soot. Bronzes not yet affected have been coated with a transparent plastic to protect them from the atmosphere, but nothing can restore the others to their beauty. To keep air pollution out, some museums have installed expensive filtration systems, but others, with the high costs involved, have been unable to do so.

Humidity is another unseen enemy. Should it remain at 70 per cent or more for as little as two hours, a bronze object with copper salts in its make-up will begin to deteriorate. Too much moisture in the air also may affect paper, cloth, and paint. Moreover, if there are wide variations in the amount of humidity, the wood panels which support so many old paintings tend to warp, crack, and buckle. The solution is careful control, removing just the right amount of moisture from the air in the summer months, adding just the right amount during colder and drier months. Ordinarily the objective is to keep humidity constant at between

40 and 50 per cent. So important a job is humidity control that in the largest museums it is one man's full-time responsibility.

One of the nagging problems of preservation involves the effect of light on paintings. The problem is strictly a modern one. In the past paintings hung in murky churches and gloomy palaces. Even the galleries to which some found their way were badly lighted. As for their protection, they were covered with coat after coat of varnish. Today the old varnish has been cleaned off and replaced with the clear nonyellowing kind. Moreover, with glass walls and glass ceilings and, often, fluorescent lighting, museums are a hundred times as bright as the old palaces and churches. Although we now get a far better look at art works, the bright light does take its toll. It may cause certain pigments to fade and thereby change the appearance of pictures. Even more serious, it is believed to speed up the aging process, weakening paintings, tapestries, and other works. Scientists working at the Mellon Institute in Pittsburgh, under the sponsorship of the National Gallery of Art, have found that the most destructive light rays in museums are the ultraviolet and have urged that they be screened out by placing special filters over fluorescent lights, windows, and skylights.

Only a very few art museums can afford complete conservation staffs. Some may have one conservator who handles restoration of

Chief engineer William Walker examines temperature and humidity graphs reporting climatic conditions in the National Gallery of Art. *Courtesy National Gallery of Art*

paintings and any other work he can, relying where necessary on consultants. A small number have banded together to support a cooperative conservation laboratory at Oberlin College in Ohio. Other museums, with no specialist readily available, turn to consultants only as they can afford to do so. In every art museum, however, the task of preserving art works is unending. Although many museums are enormous treasure houses with thousands of priceless objects, often what they have is *all* that remains of work of a particular type. If a painting of great beauty, or a tapestry or a print or a vase, deteriorates, it cannot be replaced and man's heritage is diminished by that much.

VISITING AN ART MUSEUM

Some people approach an art museum grimly, almost as if they were approaching a shrine or taking medicine with self-improvement as their objective. More realistic goals might be enjoyment, new knowledge, and self-discovery. By looking at the world through another's eyes, particularly those of a sensitive artist, there is much one can learn about himself and the rest of the human race. A meaningful museum visit requires a responsive visitor who is willing to look and willing to see. How much knowledge you bring is, in the beginning, far less important than how open you are to ideas and how willing you are to explore. On the first few visits it makes sense simply to browse, stopping to look only at what appeals to you, returning later to see old friends and make new ones. Where a large museum is involved, it is interesting to explore the museum in detail area by area—perhaps the American prints on one afternoon, the Oriental art on another.

It is helpful to bear in mind that you don't have to like everything you see. On the other hand, it is useful to try to understand your reactions to particular works. There also is the matter of history to consider—what the work tells about how people lived and approached life hundreds or thousands of years ago. By seeing the art objects owned by members of the ruling class in France just prior to the French Revolution, it is easier to understand the frivolous excesses that led to their downfall. By seeing portraits of the most important persons involved, it is easier to know them as individuals. In the same way, Egyptian art offers an account of how people lived as well as a record of their creative achievements.

There are, of course, many kinds of art works you will encounter. With those that interest you it's sound to do some background reading in guidebooks and other works to learn something of the artists involved, their objectives and techniques, and the history of the art form. It also is worthwhile to attend any gallery talks offered. As a start, the following basic approaches may be helpful. They cover paintings, prints, sculpture, Egyptian art, armor, and period rooms.

Paintings. A good system for learning something of paintings is contrasting two paintings of a similar type—perhaps two portraits or two landscapes. Start with the subject and try to define what kind of a reaction you have when you look at each picture. Also consider what the artist's attitude toward his subject is in each case. In the portraits "Count Pelegrino" by Jean Ingres and "First Madame Millet" by Jean Millet, on page 99, the contrast is quite clear. The Ingres painting is intellectual, formal, reserved, almost detached; whereas the Millet, a portrait of his wife, is emotional and involves the viewer to a greater extent.

It also is interesting to consider colors, brush strokes, and lines and shapes an artist uses. All contribute to the effect a picture has. Thus, circular forms give a picture a soft, feminine quality; rectangular forms help create an air of stability; diagonals convey a sense of action. Johannes Vermeer's famous painting, "Young Woman with a Water Jug" on page 100, is a good example of the effect of line and form. The many rectangles—the window, the map on the wall, the walls themselves—help create a mood of cool, ordered tranquillity. The clear light with which the room is suffused, the crisp details of the objects, and the woman's expression also contribute to this effect.

A painting by Camille Pissarro, "Boulevard des Italiens, Morning, Sunlight," on page 101, is interesting to study for its brush-

Top: "First Madame Millet,"
by Jean Millet. Bottom:
"Count Pelegrino," by Jean
Ingres. *Courtesy Art Institute
of Chicago*

The rectangles in "Young Woman with a Water Jug" by Johannes Vermeer create a mood of cool, ordered tranquility. *Metropolitan Museum of Art: gift of Henry G. Marquand, 1889*

work and color. Pissarro was a French Impressionist painter who, like some members of that school, applied small dabs of different colors one next to another with the objective of showing the effect of light. At a distance the bits of color seem to blend. In this picture the scene is a busy Paris boulevard of the late nineteenth century as seen in the early morning from Pissarro's hotel room.

A painting by Antoine Watteau, another French artist, is an example of the ways an artist may organize his work. In "Italian Comedians," on page 101, the clown obviously is the central figure. His position in the painting, his white costume, the contrasting red costumes nearby, the man introducing him on the right, and the spiral of figures on the left all carry the viewer's eye to him. Watteau indicates his characters as actors in a comedy through the use of the smiling mask immediately above the clown's head.

With modern painting one encounters a confusing variety of styles and approaches. In the broadest terms, however, there are three categories involved. One is the realistic painting, dealing with things as they appear to the eye. Another is the abstraction in

Top: "Boulevard des Italiens, Morning, Sunlight" by Camille Pissaro.
Bottom: "Italian Comedians" by Antoine Watteau. *Courtesy National Gallery of Art*

which the artist takes something that is real and changes it in a way which reflects his feelings about it. The third category is the nonobjective. It is an exercise in the arrangement of space and color.

Pablo Picasso's painting "Guernica," shown below, is a good example of an abstraction. The subject of the painting is the saturation bombing of the population of the Spanish town of Guernica during the Spanish Civil War. It was the first time in history that civilians had been wantonly attacked in this way. Through the use of exaggeration and the colors of mourning—black, white, and gray—Picasso expresses his feelings of horror and outrage. One can recognize the figures he has painted, but in each case they have been distorted to reflect the dreadful distortion of life, dignity, and feeling that had taken place. At the left, an anguished, screaming mother carries her dead child. At the center, a horse dies, his entrails spilling onto the ground. At the top of the picture the jagged lines underscore the harshness of the scene. At the right, a woman with a lamp peers with shock and disbelief from a window.

Another kind of abstraction is a work the artist Robert Rauschenberg describes as a "combine painting" in which he

"Guernica" by Pablo Picasso. *Collection, The Museum of Modern Art, New York*

combines a number of familiar materials. The combine painting, shown below, is called "First Landing Jump." It represents Rauschenberg's idea of the American landscape. His materials, all from the landscape, include a tire, a street lamp shield, a rusty 1959 Connecticut license plate, part of a shirt, part of a fence, a little cloth bag, and a lighted blue bulb. The first reaction of a viewer may be that he simply threw these materials together. But

"First Landing Jump" by Robert Rauschenberg. *Collection, The Museum of Modern Art, New York*

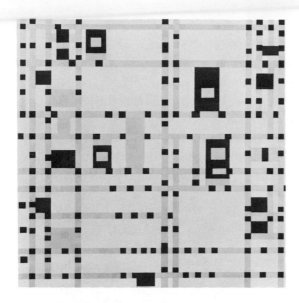

"Broadway Boogie Woogie" by Piet Mondrian. *Collection, The Museum of Modern Art, New York*

if one studies the work for a few minutes, he finds there is a kind of flow and order to the arrangement. For example, Rauschenberg uses the strong lines of the fence post as directional signals to the eye. The downward thrust of the rust spot on the light shield also is used in this way.

"Broadway Boogie Woogie," shown above, by the Dutch artist Piet Mondrian, is an example of a nonobjective painting. In the 1940's when he was seventy Mondrian came to New York and promptly was fascinated by the boogie woogie style in jazz and by the lights in Times Square. Although the painting represents neither Times Square nor jazz, a sense of both is present. His primary objective was to divide his canvas into an interesting arrangement of rectangles and squares which he then painted with the primary colors: red, blue, and yellow. The picture looks as if it was easy to do, but it wasn't. Mondrian spent a great deal of time adjusting slips of paper until he had achieved the right arrangement. In addition, the vertical and horizontal lines in the picture seem to be the same width, but were deliberately varied. The result is a painting with a great deal of movement; indeed, some of the squares look like blinking lights. With the title as a clue, one well may see a resemblance to Times Square perhaps on a rainy night with reflections of light bouncing off a wet pavement. Although Mondrian's work was purely an artistic effort, it has had an important influence on modern advertising, architecture, and industrial design.

Prints. A print literally is anything which is printed from a surface that has been inked. Such a surface might be type or it might be a wood block, a stone, or metal plate. In artistic terms, a print is a work created by an artist who places it on a printing surface, using techniques described later, and then either prints the work himself or supervises its printing. Modern practice is to print a number of copies of a work, then destroy the plate or block from which the copies were made. The artist inspects the proofs as they are pulled and signs and numbers each one that meets his standards. Although there may be as many as two hundred copies of a given print, each is regarded as an original in that it has come directly from the artist's hand. Because prints are produced in multiple editions, there is a tendency to regard them as lesser works of art. However, many are creations of great beauty and also of considerable value. Only a few years ago, for example, a Rembrandt print brought $72,000 at auction. For a print to be in a museum, it must be regarded either as a work of art or as an illustration of historical or social interest. Some museums have broad collections which take in both types of prints. Thus the collection at the Philadelphia Museum of Art includes great masterpieces and also illustrations of such varied subjects as table settings, medical techniques, early efforts to reach the moon, and Philadelphia streets which no longer exist. In all, there are over 100,000 prints in the museum's collection. Even larger collections, all with this broad focus, are at the New York Public Library, the Metropolitan Museum of Art, and the Museum of Fine Arts in Boston. On the other hand, at New York's Museum of Modern Art, the emphasis is only on prints of the very highest artistic quality and the collection there consists of but eight thousand items. However, even small print collections hardly are "small" when measured against the size of other museum collections; in fact, they usually surpass the size of all other collections together.

What also is intriguing are the techniques used in print-making. The oldest form is known as relief, dating to the 1400's as an artistic medium. Woodcuts and wood engravings, such as Misch Kohn's "Tiger," shown below, are in this category; so are linoleum and potato blocks. What is involved is removing a portion of the surface and printing from the raised portion that remains, as one would print from type.

Another widely used technique is intaglio. This includes engraving and etching, as well as forms known as mezzotints and aquatints. In all cases, a plate of copper or some other metal is used. The work to be printed is cut into the plate and lies below the surface instead of above the surface. In engraving, the artist or craftsman cuts into the plate with an engraver's tool. In etching, a corrosive such as acid is used to eat away areas of the metal plate. When the plate is inked, the ink lies in the hollows rather than on the surface. When the print is produced, the ink is literally pulled out of the crevices and sits on top of the paper, resulting in a

"Tiger" by Misch Kohn, a woodcut. *Philadelphia Museum of Art, Print Club Permanent Collection*

"Spring" by Pieter Brueghel, an etching. *Philadelphia Museum of Art: gift of Henry P. McIlhenny*

raised quality. On the other hand, the relief technique leaves a flat surface. Pieter Brueghel's "Spring," shown above, is an example of an etching.

The third major technique in use is lithography. Lithographs do not involve cutting. Instead, they are printed from a finely grained limestone or a specially prepared sheet of zinc. The artist draws directly on the printing surface with a greasy crayon known as a *tusche;* the rest of the surface is dampened with water. When the ink is applied, it is attracted to the grease and repelled by the water, so that only the greased area prints. This was the method used to print "The Jockey" by Henri de Toulouse-Lautrec, on page 108. Other techniques also are used from time to time, including

"The Jockey" by Henri de Toulouse-Lautrec, a lithograph. *Philadelphia Museum of Art*

stencil and silk screen. In the latter, which frequently is used with Japanese prints, pigment is forced through those portions of a piece of fine mesh silk not covered with a stencil. At least one twentieth-century artist, Caroline Durieux, has made "electron" prints with ink she loaded with radioactive isotopes. First she made her drawing in the treated ink, then she made copies by placing photo-sensitive paper on top of the drawing. The result was a print with a photographic quality. Since the treated ink was dangerous, she worked in rubber gloves and a mask.

Artists select techniques in terms of their subjects and the effects they wish to achieve. The lithographic process, for example, is very free; with intaglio, on the other hand, a crisp, clear effect is achieved.[13]

[13] This discussion is based on an interview with Kneeland McNulty, curator of prints and drawings at the Philadelphia Museum of Art.

Sculpture. Although the objective of the sculptor is no different from that of the painter or the printmaker, his techniques, materials, and results all are radically different. He may cut into and carve away such materials as marble, granite, alabaster, ivory, or wood. Often the result is a three-dimensional figure to be viewed from all sides. When he works in relief, carving into a piece of stone or metal, as he might in the side of a building, what he creates only can be seen from the front. In other cases he may model in clay, building up, rather than cutting away. Then he may make a mold of his work and from it produce casts, in bronze or some other metal, just as a printmaker produces editions of his original work. Casts of the famous statue "The Thinker" by Auguste Rodin, shown below, are displayed in the United States in such places as the Detroit Institute of Arts, the Rodin Museum in Philadelphia, the Cleveland Museum of Art, and the California Palace of the Legion of Honor in San Francisco. Look closely and you will see the impressions left in the clay by Rodin's fingers and tools. As with some contemporary painters, sculptors also may work in abstract and nonobjective forms. Constantin Brancusi's "Bird in Space," page 110, is a good example, showing neither bird nor flight but somehow the underlying nature of both. The

Cast of "The Thinker"
by Auguste Rodin.
*Courtesy Detroit Institute
of Arts*

modern artist also may construct sculpture, often out of metal. A remarkable example on display at the Metropolitan Museum of Art in New York is "The Sun" by Richard Lippold, shown below, which is made of gold wire, and is 11 feet high and 22 feet wide.

Egyptian Art.   One of the reasons Egyptian art fascinates so many people, particularly young people, is its antiquity. Many of the Egyptian objects now in museums have survived for five thousand years in dry sand or air-tight tombs. Another reason is the hieroglyphics, the strange writing that puzzled scholars for so long and that almost everyone who visits an Egyptian gallery tries to translate. The translations of the few hieroglyphs on page 111 give an idea of how the symbols worked, but bear in mind that hundreds were in use.

Still another reason for Egypt's appeal is the mummies, the dead preserved for thousands of years by embalming—not only humans, but birds, cats, dogs, and other creatures. When mummies are shown, however, it is not because *they* are works of

Left: "Bird in Space" by Constantin Brancusi. *Collection, The Museum of Modern Art, New York.* Right: "The Sun" by Richard Lippold. *Courtesy Metropolitan Museum of Art: photograph, Gary Winograd*

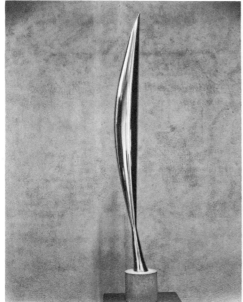

AN EGYPTIAN HIEROGLYPHIC ALPHABET

of 2500 B.C.

WHAT THE HIEROGLYPHS REPRESENT

The signs were usually given the natural coloring of the objects they represent, in several hues. But they were often uniformly colored blue or green, especially on monuments containing religious texts.

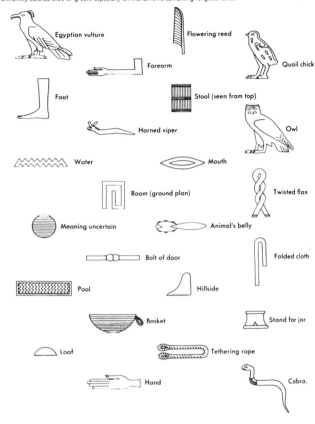

Egyptian vulture · Flowering reed · Forearm · Quail chick · Foot · Stool (seen from top) · Horned viper · Owl · Water · Mouth · Room (ground plan) · Twisted flax · Meaning uncertain · Animal's belly · Bolt of door · Folded cloth · Pool · Hillside · Basket · Stand for jar · Loaf · Tethering rope · Hand · Cobra.

HOW THE HIEROGLYPHS SOUNDED

ꜣ (aleph)* · y · '('ayin)* · w · b · p · f · m · n · r · h · emphatic h* · ch (as in Loch Lomond) · ch (closer to sh) · z · s · sh · q (at back of throat)* · k · g · t · tch (as in catch) · d · dj

HOW THE HIEROGLYPHS WERE USED

The ancient Egyptians used hieroglyphs for monuments and religious documents. They also had a more flowing kind of writing for everyday use, like our script. The hieroglyphs shown here are only a few of the several hundred signs that made up the entire Egyptian system of writing. But these alphabetic signs (each representing only a single sound) were used more repeatedly than most of the others (some of which represented a group of sounds, or an entire word). Although the Egyptians themselves never simplified their hieroglyphic writing so as to use the alphabetic signs alone, this possibility was realized by their eastern neighbors in Sinai and the coast of Syria, who created the ancestor of our own alphabet. Like the Egyptian writing that inspired it, this ancestral alphabet contained only consonants. The invention of vowel signs only came about when the Greeks in turn borrowed the alphabetic system from the Phoenicians.

WRITING YOUR NAME IN HIEROGLYPHS

For those who wish to try writing their names in hieroglyphs, or their friends' names, it may help to use 🕊 for w or oo and 𝄀𝄀 for i or y. There is no l in ancient Egyptian, but it can be expressed by ∿∿(n).

EXAMPLES: ▢𝄀𝄀 Peter · Jim · ▢∿∿ Helen · Sue

* This sound does not exist in English.

Courtesy Metropolitan Museum of Art

art or particularly interesting in their own right, but because the cases they occupy are beautiful. Seeing a mummy in a mummy case makes it easier to understand why such cases were created and what they looked like when in use. But one also gets the impression that some museums show mummies in deference to the interests of their younger visitors.

If one can judge by the Brooklyn Museum's experience of some years ago, it is easier to display a mummy than to get rid of it. It had in its possession a mummy dating to 350 A.D. which was of interest because it had no case but only a simple cloth wrapping and fastened to it a decorated face and chest cloth known as a *cartonnage*. The cartonnage was of interest because it showed how Egyptian interest in elaborate burial customs had changed and how, in fact, Egyptian society had declined over the centuries. While the cartonnage, as shown below, had historical and artistic value, the dried, fleshless body of the mummy had absolutely none. Thus the museum decided to dispose of it. One of the workmen assigned to the job objected. The museum was destroying "the body of a person of the Christian era with an immortal soul," he declared. In deference to this belief, the museum decided to have the mummy buried in a Brooklyn cemetery. However, cemetery officials said a burial permit was needed, and this could not be obtained until a death certificate was issued which, in turn,

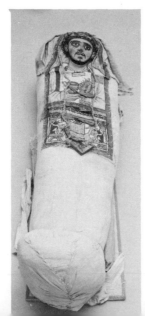

The cartonnage of Melvin the mummy. *Courtesy The Brooklyn Museum*

could not be issued until the cause of death was determined—which was impossible. Then it was suggested that the mummy be sent to a small museum outside New York, but without a death certificate a body—any body—cannot be moved across state lines. The museum's plight was reported on a TV show and later in *Life* magazine, with the result that requests for the mummy, by now known as Melvin, came in from all over. Warner Brothers wanted it for a movie. Cherokee, Iowa, wanted it to help put Cherokee on the map. A librarian in Kentucky wanted it to fill a long, empty shelf. A couple of embalmers wanted it for any number of reasons. In exchange for the mummy, a Chicago mail clerk offered a Hebrew prayer book, while Odessa, Texas, offered Southwestern artifacts. In the end the Brooklyn Museum decided to keep the mummy and displayed it as part of an exhibit on burial customs and art. When the show was over, the mummy was tucked away in a storeroom where it remains today.[14]

At least as intriguing as mummies are Egyptian drawings and paintings. Most of those displayed in museums once adorned the walls of tombs. They were not decorations but highly practical illustrated records. The Egyptians believed in a form of life after death. The tomb drawings were to assist the spirit of the person who occupied the tomb in regaining a satisfactory life. It was believed that once the soul escaped the body, the drawings would become real and inscriptions on the walls would become facts of life. Understandably a majority of the drawings relate to food. They show animals being bred and butchered, and food being planted, harvested, stored, and eaten. But others relate to other aspects of life it was assumed would continue, such as favorite games one would play and conversations he would hold. Statues, furniture, clothing, and implements left in tombs served the same purpose.[15]

[14] *Junior Membership Bulletin of the Brooklyn Museum.* Vol. 2, No. 2.
[15] Dunham, *The Egyptian Department and Its Excavations.* Museum of Fine Arts, Boston.

To modern eyes the drawings are particularly strange. They are flat, two-dimensional, and make no use of perspective. This didn't bother the Egyptians, however, since their objective was not to depict reality. Instead it was to depict what was in a scene even if what was shown was not visible in a real situation because of where one stood. An interesting example of the differences between this approach and the one used today is shown in the drawings on pages 115 and 116, which were developed by Dows Dunham, curator emeritus of Egyptian Art at Boston's Museum of Fine Arts. Mr. Dunham suggests we imagine a walled enclosure with doorways in the center of two adjoining sides. Inside the enclosure are two palm trees, each of which is surrounded by two small mud dikes. A pool stands at the center of the enclosure in which swim a fish and a duck. An artist of ancient Egypt would present the scene as it is shown in the top drawing. A modern-day artist, however, simply could not show everything in one picture. His drawing very likely would resemble the lower one. The Egyptians also took such liberties in drawing human figures. Thus, all faces are shown in profile since this provides the best view of noses, mouths, and chins. Because an eye is incomplete in profile, however, it is included as it would look from the front. For the same reason, shoulders and the upper half of the body are drawn as seen from the front. On the other hand, the female bosom is presented in profile because it is more completely represented in this way. The two drawings on page 116 show the difference between the Egyptian and Western approaches. The drawing at the top represents a scene that appears on a wall of the tomb of Queen Meresankh III at Giza. The queen and her mother, accompanied by a young boy, are plucking stalks of papyrus while a boatman keeps the craft steady. All four figures are represented in curiously mixed profiles which include both side and front views. In addition, the women are oversized and the male figures undersized to give a sense of their relative importance. The lower scene, drawn by Suzanne E. Chapman, artist-technician at the Museum of Fine Arts, illustrates the approach a modern artist would use.

Top: A walled garden as an ancient Egyptian would have drawn it.
Bottom: The same garden as a modern artist might draw it. *Courtesy
Museum of Fine Arts, Boston*

Top: A scene from the wall of the tomb of Queen Meresankh III. Bottom: The same scene as reproduced by a modern-day artist. *Courtesy Museum of Fine Arts, Boston*

Armor. Although one may not think of a suit of armor as a work of art, the armor found in museums is just that. It is a form of sculpture in steel created by armorers who in their day ranked with other artists. In addition, many suits of armor are decorated with precious metals and are beautifully engraved, etched, or embossed. The photograph of the parade armor on page 117 is an example of this. In a sense, such armor represented the finest and most expensive "jewelry" one could buy. And it was very costly. It is said that Emperor Charles V of the Holy Roman Empire paid more for his armor than the great painter Titian received for his portraits. Most of the armor one sees in museums was custom-made, and much of it was used for ceremonial purposes or for tournaments. The specialized armor used in tournaments sometimes weighed as much as one hundred pounds. On the other hand, the field armor used in battle weighed, on the average, between fifty-five and sixty-five pounds. Ceremonial armor was

Detail from the breast plate of Henry II of France, about 1550. *Metropolitan Museum of Art: Dick Fund, 1939*

lightest of all, since its defensive abilities were of secondary importance.

The widespread use of plate armor was relatively brief. It did not appear as a complete body defense until the second half of the fourteenth century when the crossbow was improved and something more solid was needed to prevent penetration than the mail armor then in use. Mail consisted of interlinking steel rings riveted closed to form a flexible mesh. By the seventeenth century, however, plate armor itself was outmoded as a result of the increased use of firearms, but it continued to serve for ceremonial purposes. The modern descendants of armor are, of course, the steel helmet and the bulletproof vest. In fact, the helmet the modern American soldier wears derives from a number of experimental helmets the Department of Arms and Armor at the Metropolitan Museum of Art designed for the U.S. Army.

In studying a suit of armor, it is well to first determine what you are looking at—whether it is ceremonial, tournament, or field armor. It also is interesting to determine whose armor it was, since the owner probably was an important man. Then consider its shape, the efficiency of its design, its ornamentation, and the craftsmanship required for its construction. Any dents or holes you see may be difficult to explain. If it is tournament armor, a lance may have been responsible. Curators sometimes can tell this by the kind of dent that resulted. But if it is field armor used in battle, the cause is more difficult to pin down. One suggestion. Don't look for the plate armor the Crusaders wore; except for their helmets, they had none. Instead their bodies were protected by shirts of mail worn over padded garments, and none of these shirts is known to have survived intact. Suits of armor often are displayed on wooden mannequins with hinged joints. If a mannequin is too small for a suit of armor, it may be enlarged through the use of a papier-mâché form suggesting the size of the man who wore the armor.

Collections of armor often include collections of weapons, such as daggers, swords, crossbows, and firearms. What qualifies them as art are their beautiful decorations. The finest collection of arms and armor in the United States is at the Metropolitan Museum of Art in New York, which includes almost fifteen thousand items, perhaps 10 per cent of which is on display. The other major American collection is at the John Woodman Higgins Armory of the Worcester Pressed Steel Company in Worcester, Massachusetts. However, many large art museums in the United States and Canada have at least a few pieces on display.[16]

Period Rooms. A period room is essentially just that—a room representing a period in history. Ordinarily much or all of such a room—that is, its walls, floors, doors, carvings and moldings, fireplaces and mantels, and possibly its ceiling—has been moved from the building it originally occupied to a museum where it has been reconstructed. Then it has been authentically furnished so that the room reflects a style of living that prevailed at the time it was built. Art museums and history museums both have period rooms. Where they differ is in emphasis. The art museum is concerned primarily with the art of decoration: the architecture, the interior design, and the furnishings used. Usually its rooms are examples of elegance and beauty. The history museum's major interest is social history: how people of all types lived and how their homes reflected their lives, tastes, values, and concerns. Thus the crude, rude, and tasteless also may be shown. In either case, period rooms usually are purchased as a unit, either from the owner of a house as it is being dismantled or from a dealer.

The period room made its first appearance in American museums in the 1920's at the Philadelphia Museum of Art. The largest collection in the United States today is at the remarkable Henry Francis du Pont Winterthur Museum outside Wilmington, Delaware. It possesses over 125 beautifully furnished rooms, along with a glorious free-hanging spiral stairway from a house near

[16] This account is drawn in part from an interview at the Metropolitan Museum of Art with the curator of arms and armor, Randolph Bullock, and the associate curator, Helmut Nickel.

Warrenton, North Carolina, and countless halls, passages, and alcoves. Taken together they provide a magnificently illustrated history of decorative arts in the United States. Other art museums with period rooms include the Metropolitan Museum, Boston's Museum of Fine Arts, the Brooklyn Museum, the Detroit Institute of Arts, the Denver Art Museum, and the Minneapolis Institute of Arts. Two of the pleasantest rooms at the Minneapolis museum come from a house that was built for Colonel John Stuart at the corner of Tradd and Orange streets in Charleston, South Carolina. One is Colonel Stuart's dining room; the other is his sitting room. They are immensely spacious rooms—open, cool, obviously designed for a warm, damp climate. Moreover, their furnishings—the Oriental rugs, the china from England, a chandelier of Venetian glass, objects carved of ivory—reflect the romance of a seaport such as Charleston to which ships come from far-off places.

Although some museum people regard period rooms as prized possessions, others are not so sure. They complain that rooms taken from their original surroundings look less like rooms that people once used than like dull museum pieces. However, some museums do go to considerable lengths to give their period rooms a sense of occupancy. At Winterthur there are freshly cut flowers in many of the rooms, and the lamps, chandeliers, and candelabra give off a soft glow through the use of hundreds of tiny candle-flame bulbs. In Minneapolis, playing cards are laid out on a whist table, and a decanter of wine (actually tea) stands ready for use. In Hartford, Connecticut, at the Wadsworth Atheneum, at least one period room is home to a mannequin costumed in the dress of the period. Among the most successful of such attempts are the five dozen miniature period rooms that have become a landmark of the Art Institute of Chicago. Devised by the late Mrs. James Ward Thorne, the rooms provide histories of European and American interior design. Although but one-twelfth the size of the rooms they represent, they are remarkably realistic. Many offer views out of windows and into hallways. All are furnished with beautifully

Top: An upper-class dining room of the first half of the 19th century at the Winterthur Museum. *Courtesy The Henry Francis du Pont Winterthur Museum*. Bottom: 16th century French bedroom. The room is a miniature, but 1/12th the size of the room it represents. *From the Thorne Rooms: Courtesy Art Institute of Chicago*

crafted miniature reproductions of furniture, carpeting, lamps, and other furnishings. Some of the most fascinating are miniature books in which even the text is to scale.

Perhaps the best advice on visiting a period room is to study detail and make comparisons. For example, look closely at the furniture, its coverings, its size and scale, and consider how comfortable it might be; also examine the carpeting and the draperies, the detail in the woodwork, the types of lighting and the kinds of pictures and books. Then compare the room you are visiting with other period rooms you have seen and with a room used for a similar purpose in your own home.

3 | History Muscums

A FEW DAYS BEFORE THIS WAS WRITTEN, I READ IN THE NEWSPAPER that a group of 157 people, from California to Nova Scotia, were trying to buy a weatherbeaten ninety-four-year-old railroad station at North Canaan, Connecticut. At one time the station was a magnificent building. The group wanted to restore it to the way it was when it was first built, and then turn it into a railroad museum. Earlier in the same week, I had read that Beale Street in Memphis, Tennessee, the home of the blues, had been named a National Historic Landmark by the Federal government. The preceding month, in Millstone, New Jersey, an old forge, where George Washington once had his horses shod, was dedicated as a museum. At about the same time, Pete Seeger, the folk singer,

raised $1,500 at a concert to help build a floating museum that would sail up and down New York's Hudson River and carry the story of the early settlers to people who live in the river valley today. About a month before the concert the Grandma Moses Museum, dedicated to the memory of the famous artist, received its first visitors in the old one-room school it occupies in Eagle Bridge, New York.

Although no one has precise figures, it is estimated that there are about 2,500 history museums of all types in the United States. What is startling is the rate at which they increase. On the average at least one new history museum opens in the country every week. What is equally remarkable is the range of subjects they deal with. The very largest, the Smithsonian's Museum of History and Technology in Washington, D.C., is concerned with the broad sweep of national history. Some deal with the histories of particular regions, states, cities, towns, events, and men. Others are concerned with the history of maritime life, aircraft, trolley cars, money, stamps, Boy Scouts, Negroes, medicine, fire-fighting, fur-trading, jazz, law enforcement, dolls, baseball, and, very likely, almost any other subject that might occur to you. Together, as the historian Fred Rath points out, they make up a remarkable mosaic of American history from the earliest Indian times to the present, each contributing its story to the overall story of the nation's growth and development.

Some of these museums are excellent. Through intensive research and imaginative techniques, they provide an accurate, interesting, often exciting and moving sense of the past. At times, one comes away from such places not only with new knowledge, but with a feeling of renewed pride in man's achievements. However, not all history museums can be as helpful. Many are among the nation's newest museums and are handicapped by severe shortages of money and trained personnel. In fact, it is the amateur historian who continues to be responsible for the operation of many of the smaller history museums. Some do quite a good job, but one sees enough poor and pointless museums to wonder whether all the new ones really are necessary. New history museums—good and bad—continue to appear, however, and attendance continues to rise. It is estimated that at present over 100 million visits a year are made to history museums. Often visitors travel out of their way to reach them, and once they arrive, pay substantial admission fees.

Why this great interest? One can cite all the reasons for the popularity of all museums—that people have more leisure, more money, and more education—and then add two more. One is the car. Some history museums are in downtown locations, but the largest number are in the countryside and the suburbs where the event they are concerned with took place or where the people involved in their story lived and worked. The only practical way to reach these "roadside museums" is by driving. Until the family car became commonplace in the 1920's and 1930's, such museums had relatively few visitors or did not exist. George Washington's home in Mount Vernon, Virginia, is a case in point. It is but sixteen miles from the nation's capital, yet before automobile ownership became widespread visitors in a busy year might be counted in the thousands. In 1966 cars and buses traveling over the George Washington Memorial Parkway brought more than 1.3 million people to Mount Vernon.

Another reason for the history museum's popularity is said to be a desire for "roots." Although everyone wants to know about the past, historians believe the need is particularly pressing in a country as big, as new, and as complex as the United States where things change fast, people move often, and family groups are small. Seeing oneself as part of a continuing procession in history, knowing the national heroes and the great events, understanding how ordinary people lived and worked—all this, it is said, gives one a sense of belonging. There also is another reason for the popularity of some history museums, but it has more to do with entertainment than with history. It is that some museums, particularly the re-created towns and villages, are fun to visit. There may be stagecoaches, paddlewheel boats, and old cars to ride in, forts to explore, craftsmen and "natives" in costume to observe, parades to watch, and good things to eat. Whether life actually was as pleasant as it is shown is open to question, but that visitors have a good time and flock to such places is clear.

The primary role of the history museum is to preserve and interpret. It preserves a record of man's development, experiences, and ideas as well as his values—what he saw as important and worthwhile in life. This information is acquired in the form of written documents, objects, clothing, rooms, buildings, entire towns.

A few history museums are deeply involved in historical research. But a surprising number do little or no research and have few, if any, collections of interest to the scholar. In such museums, the sole concern is with displaying objects and presenting facts, and through them telling the story of a period, an event, or a man. As a result, when one refers to a "history museum" he may be describing a traditional museum which, if it is large enough, has curatorial departments, or a historic building that has been preserved, or an outdoor museum of restored, reconstructed, or transplanted buildings, or a battlefield, or a historic neighborhood, or a commercial wax museum where wax and plastic figures depict noteworthy and not so noteworthy moments in history, or a sound-and-light presentation where tape recordings, film, and lights are used to re-create military campaigns and other events.

BEGINNINGS

The first history museum in the United States may well have been the modest collection of portraits, documents, and artifacts that an amateur historian, Pierre du Simitière, assembled in his home in Philadelphia in the early 1780's. However, the movement to systematically assemble such material and keep continuous historical records had its roots in Boston, where in 1791 the Massachusetts Historical Society was founded, and in New York, where in 1804 the New-York Historical Society came into being. In turn, still other historical societies were established, usually by amateurs. Some were statewide in their interests; others were concerned with a county or with a city or a town. In every case their purpose was to collect and preserve documents and other records that would tell the story of the developments of their area. Many of the documents they assembled were written. Others were three-dimensional, such as furniture, clothing, tools, and agricultural implements. These ultimately served as the basis of museums.

The first of the many historic houses preserved in the United States today were acquired as museums in the 1850's. One was George Washington's mansion at Mount Vernon. His great-grandnephew, John Augustine Washington, had offered it for $200,000 to the Federal government, which declined it. He then offered it to the Commonwealth of Virginia, which also declined it. To save the house a South Carolina woman named Ann Pamela Cunningham organized the Mount Vernon Ladies' Association of the Union and by 1858 raised the money needed. Today the ownership is unchanged, as is the objective: "To perpetuate the sacred memory of 'The Father of His Country' and, with loving hands, to guard and protect the hallowed spot where rest his mortal remains." The other historic house was a stone farmhouse in Newburgh, New York, which Washington used as a headquarters in 1782–83 and where he announced the end of the Revolutionary War, rejected a suggestion that he become king, and created the Order of the Purple Heart. The State of New York acquired the farmhouse in 1851 and still operates it.

The Smithsonian's Museum of History and Technology in Washington, D.C., which later became known as the "nation's attic," was opened to visitors in 1879. Its first acquisitions were the exhibits that thirty countries had maintained at the grand and glorious Philadelphia Centennial Exposition three years before. Twenty-one freight cars were needed to haul the assorted riches to Washington. To house them, Congress quickly provided a new building, which today is the Arts and Industries Building. However, the natural history museum also was to share the quarters. The result was a wild confusion of stuffed animals, dinosaur skeletons, locomotives, Army uniforms, and industrial equipment. Only in 1911, when the natural history displays were moved to their own building, did the history museum move from chaos to order and begin to faintly resemble the important museum it is today.[1]

Two other events in this period also were forerunners of important future developments. In 1910 the Society for the Preservation of New England Antiquities was established in Boston as the first major organization concerned with rescuing historic buildings from destruction. In 1913 the Norwegian-American Museum of Decorah, Iowa, moved a pioneer log cabin six miles to its headquarters and thereby began what was to grow into the nation's first outdoor museum. The end of World War I saw a marked increase in the number of history museums. One of the most important to be established was Colonial Williamsburg. It was in 1926 that John D. Rockefeller, Jr., a major supporter of the Metropolitan Museum of Art, became interested in restoring the Virginia city to its eighteenth century appearance. The man who conceived the idea and convinced Rockefeller to pursue it was a minister, the Rev. William A. R. Goodwin, rector of the Bruton Parish Church in Williamsburg. The project began in 1927 and still is in progress. To date over $74 million has been spent in restoring and reconstructing a 130-acre area about a mile long and a half-mile wide. The techniques being used are described later in this chapter. One Williamsburg official estimates that the project may not be completed until the 1980's.

As work was beginning at Williamsburg, two important collectors were searching out American crafts and folk art that later would serve as the basis for other major history museums. One of the collectors was Electra Havemeyer Webb, whose parents, the H. O. Havemeyers, had given their magnificent art treasures to the Metropolitan Museum. Mrs. Webb's collections would become in

[1] Karp, *The Smithsonian Institution,* pp. 76–78.

1952 the substance of the Shelburne Museum, near Shelburne, Vermont. The other collector was A. B. Wells, a Southbridge, Massachusetts, industrialist whose acquisitions led to the formation in 1936 of Old Sturbridge Village. Meanwhile, in 1929, a doctor, a lawyer, and an industrialist, distressed by the destruction of irreplaceable maritime relics and records, formed a nonprofit educational organization to gather and protect such materials. The result in later years was another famous New England museum, Mystic Seaport in Mystic, Connecticut. In the same year, Henry Ford's personal monument to American history, the Henry Ford Museum and Greenfield Village, had its beginning in Dearborn, Michigan.

Starting in the 1930's the Federal government took a number of steps which had two important effects on history museums. One was to increase the number of good museums. The other was to help expand the idea of a history museum to include important historic sites, not only irreplaceable buildings, but also historic streets, neighborhoods, battlefields, and cemeteries which needed preservation and care just as important objects in a museum do. This was not a new idea, but the government's interest in historic preservation caused a great deal to be done that otherwise might never have taken place. The first step, in 1933, was a decision to make the National Park Service responsible for preserving and interpreting the most important historic sites. So effective has the program been that by 1967 the Park Service was operating over a hundred sites, from an Indian mission in Walla Walla, Washington, to the late President Franklin D. Roosevelt's home in Hyde Park, New York. In each case there are displays or full-fledged museums to explain the importance of what is preserved. In 1933 the Historic American Buildings Survey also was organized. Its purpose was to establish a badly needed architectural record of the nation's important historic buildings. Thus far, photographs, records, and measured drawings have been prepared for over 10,000 structures, information particularly useful to museums that want to restore or reconstruct a building.

Two years later Congress passed the Historic Sites Act which officially put the Federal government on record as supporting historic preservation. One result was a major nationwide survey through which hundreds of important sites were located, some in urgent need of care. The government purchased those sites it had funds for and strongly encouraged the states and private groups to take over the others. In 1949 Congress chartered the National Trust for Historic Preservation to provide national leadership for local and regional groups fighting to save historic sites from destruction. Operating with private funds, the Trust encourages preservation in various ways. As the need arises it also acquires and preserves important sites on its own. One of its most recent acquisitions was the Pope-Leighey House in Falls Church, Virginia, which was designed by the architect Frank Lloyd Wright. The house is of historic interest for a number of reasons. It is one of the few houses Wright created for families with modest incomes. It also contains a number of important architectural advances, such as the carport and a heated slab to replace a basement. When, in 1964, the house was threatened with destruction to make way for Interstate Highway 66, the owner asked Interior Secretary Udall for help in saving it. In turn, Udall called upon the National Trust. In the end, bulldozing was stopped until the house could be moved. Today the Trust maintains the house at Woodlawn Plantation in Virginia, another property it has responsibility for.

There are, in all, over six hundred private organizations working to save historic sites in the United States. A few are quite large, such as the Society for the Preservation of New England Antiquities which supervises over fifty properties in five states that are open to the public as museums. But most are small organizations concerned with preservation in a single city or town. The movement also has gained official backing on the local level. Over seventy cities now have Landmark Preservation Commissions with the power to designate buildings and entire neighborhoods as historic sites. Such a designation requires that the owner preserve the site as it is or, if he decides to change it, first obtain permission. As a result, owners are not always pleased when their property is so honored, and sometimes take the matter to court.

In 1960 the Federal government went one step further in behalf of preservation by establishing the Registry of National Historic Landmarks. Under this program the government singles out important historic sites and honors them, provided the owners agree to preserve them and use them appropriately. Thus far over six hundred National Historic Landmarks have been designated, including the late President Kennedy's birthplace in Boston, Sandy Hook Lighthouse off New York Harbor, and, as we have seen, Beale Street in Memphis, Tennessee. Meanwhile, of course, the number of traditional history museums has also grown and grown.

TEN BALLGOWNS FOR ONE HOUSEDRESS

The curator in charge of the new American Museum of Immigration, which is to be housed in the base of the Statue of Liberty in New York, has acquired for display a pair of shoes an immigrant wore forty years ago when he first set foot on American soil, a breakfast cloth carried to this country from Russia, and a birth certificate issued in Lithuania. As such, these objects have little value. They are neither rare nor beautiful nor were they owned by famous people nor are they terribly old. They are of interest to the curator planning the museum simply because they help tell the story of the immigrants who traveled thousands of miles to start new lives in the United States. The emphasis on ordinary things is common to all museums concerned with how people lived and what they experienced in the past. Yet, pots, pans, aprons, nightgowns, horse collars, toothbrushes, and the other stuff of everyday life are not always easy to come by. The reason is that the best and the finest were saved—the handsome silver, the lovely furniture, the beautiful ballgowns—but the rest often was thrown away as having no value or importance. As a result, there are some history museums that have so much finery they qualify better as museums of decorative arts. Until recent years this certainly was the case with the Museum of the City of New York, which largely reflected the life of upper-class white Protestant Episcopal New Yorkers of the nineteenth century rather than that of all New Yorkers of all periods. Yet avoiding this is not easy. "We would gladly trade ten ballgowns for one housedress," Henry D. Brown, director of the Detroit Historical Museum, told me. Reasoning in this way, Mendel Peterson, curator of armed-forces history at the Smithsonian's Museum of History and Technology and an underwater archaeologist, brought back from a recent wreck he explored a complete set of dimestore glassware made in 1961. It has been put away against the time a hundred years from now when a Smithsonian curator would treasure such a collection but find it totally impossible to obtain.

History curators also are concerned, of course, with the rare and the valuable. The inkstand used when the Declaration of Independence was signed, which is now in Independence Hall; the first plane the Wright Brothers managed to fly, which is now at the Smithsonian; the bed in which Lincoln died, which is now at the Chicago Historical Society—a chance to obtain any one of these prized objects would make any curator's heart leap with excitement.

GIFTS AND PURCHASES

Unlike the art museums, history museums ordinarily spend little on their collections, although certainly not by choice. The situation is well described by Mrs. Sutton Gustison, director of the Seattle Museum of History and Industry. "I am the biggest beggar in town," she told me. Practically nothing at her museum is purchased. Virtually everything has come to it because someone was generous, someone was seeking prestige, or someone simply had something he wanted to get rid of that seemed too valuable to throw away. Of course some of the larger museums often do have the funds to buy what they need. The Henry Ford Museum is one; Colonial Williamsburg is another. Still others may be able to raise

The square-rigger *Balclutha* on her way to her berth near the San Francisco Maritime Museum after restoration. *Courtesy San Francisco Maritime Museum: photograph, Karl Kortum*

what is needed when there is no other way. It was only by spending $150,000, for example, that the Chicago Historical Society could obtain back in the 1920's the basis of its famed collection of Lincoln objects and documents.[2] In 1954 the San Francisco Maritime Museum raised $25,000 to buy the broken-down square-rigger *Balclutha* and then convinced ninety companies and eighteen labor unions to donate $250,000 in supplies

[2] Along with the Lincoln bed, the Chicago treasures include a watch he wore, a carriage he used, chairs from the Ford Theatre where he was shot, furniture from his home in Springfield, Illinois, and a piano that was played at the White House which children visiting the museum also may play under supervision.

and labor to restore her. In recent years the Orange Empire Trolley Museum in Perris, California, also has spent well over $100,000 for old trolleys it needs to supplement those it is given. But the museum of the Minnesota Historical Society in Saint Paul is far more typical. Of the 153 acquisitions it made in 1965, only two were purchased. The rest were gifts from collectors, from ordinary citizens who contributed old farming tools, furniture, and clothing, and from the State of Minnesota which gave a group of horse collars. At the Oregon Historical Society in Portland, many gifts are personal items which were owned by pioneers and donated by their children and grandchildren.

At times the gifts a museum receives are truly splendid. In 1965, for example, the Smithsonian Museum of History and Technology was given outstanding collections of water meters, time-keeping devices, and phonographs, along with a 1917 passenger bus equipped with solid rubber tires. On the other hand, not everything offered is accepted at the Smithsonian or at many other museums. There are several possible reasons for this. A museum may not collect the kind of material offered. The material may duplicate what it already has (in which case another museum may be suggested). Or an object may not be as significant or as authentic as the donor thought.

How do curators know what is authentic? Largely they rely on their knowledge of the subject. As necessary, they do research in reference books, catalogs, pattern books, old magazines, and photograph files, and they also may consult other curators. At the Dossin Great Lakes Museum in Detroit, when questionable gifts of maritime equipment arrive, the curator contacts old-time seamen who sailed the very ships from which the equipment was said to have come. But the smaller the museum and the busier the curator, the less research he can do and the more he must rely on what his experience tells him about a gift and its giver. Over the years some museums clearly have been more flexible about what they have accepted than others, either because they didn't want to offend donors or because they felt something was better than nothing. Whatever the reason, in such places one encounters a fair share of what only can be described as "junk"—broken guns, pieces of wood said to come from Old North Church in Boston or from Independence Hall, and more chairs than really seem necessary.

History museums acquire their collections in many ways. Some circulate "want lists" of items they'd like to have. Here is one such list I picked up at the Air Force Museum near Dayton, Ohio:

AIR FORCE MUSEUM
"WANT LIST"

WORLD WAR I PERIOD
Any WW I Aircraft is desired.

1919–1941 PERIOD
1. Boeing P-12
2. Boeing B-9
3. Martin B-10 or B-12
4. Seversky P-35

WORLD WAR II PERIOD
1. Bell P-39 "Airacobra"
2. Martin B-26 "Marauder"
3. Vultee BT-13 "Valiant"
4. Waco CG-4A
5. Messerschmitt 109
6. Messerschmitt 163
7. Focke Wulf 190
8. Mitsubishi "Zero"

The Air Force Museum and part of its collection of military aircraft near Dayton, Ohio. *Courtesy Air Force Museum*

Those planes with the lines through them already have been acquired. The Martin B-26, for example, was spotted from the air by an Air Force pilot flying over France. He wrote the museum about it, which in turn found that Air France was using the plane for training purposes. The museum then offered a spare DC-3 it had as a trade and the airline accepted. There are, as you see, a number of planes that are still lacking. If you know of the whereabouts of any, the museum would be glad to hear from you.

Since the estates of persons who recently died often are excellent sources of museum material, the Oregon Historical Society has a staff member who regularly checks the obituary pages and notes anyone who had important pioneer, social, or business connections. Then the survivors are sent a letter which tells of the museum's interest. "This is a critical time to write you," the letter reads, "but often this is the moment when important, irreplaceable memorabilia are destroyed. This is your great Western historical institution. . . . If you have letters, diaries, photographs, and negatives, paintings, business records, or museum articles such as tools, furniture, or other equipment, please telephone or write us. . . ."

Almost 90 per cent of the fascinating collection of early farm equipment at the Farmers' Museum in Cooperstown, New York, also was acquired simply by asking. The man who did the asking was George Campbell who today is curator of the museum. But in those days during World War II the museum did not yet exist. Mr. Campbell was instructed to go around and make friends with farmers in the area and see what he could find. He simply leaned over the fence, started talking with the friends he'd made about a Farmers' Museum that was going to be opened after the war, and asked if they didn't have stuff in their barns and attics they'd like to give.

Another curator, this one from the Smithsonian's Museum of History and Technology, spent months searching the northern California countryside for an authentic settler's kitchen which had been used in the period after the Gold Rush. If he could find one, it would be installed in the museum's Hall of Everyday Life in the American Past. But century-old kitchens of this sort are not easy to come by. He visited museums large and small, as well as historical societies and antique shops, but no one he talked with knew of such a room. The best he could do was acquire here and there what seemed to be the proper furnishings. Two years passed. A California woman heard about his project and took him to an abandoned ranch house her great-grandfather, George Washington Arbaugh, a gold miner and rancher, had built in 1862 at the foot of Mount Shasta in Siskiyou County. It was a two-room house, and one of the rooms was a kitchen. Could the Smithsonian take the room back to Washington? Permission granted, the kitchen was photographed, measured, taken apart, shipped to the museum, reassembled, furnished with the curator's earlier acquisitions, and put on display.[3]

In seeking gifts, however, a museum sometimes may get far more than it bargained for. The biggest cross one of the maritime museums has to bear is a steam engine from the frigate *Ranger,* one of the Navy's first steam frigates. When the museum learned that the *Ranger* was being scrapped, its officials asked for the engine and the Navy agreed to let them have it. Soon after, the museum received a call from a nearby Navy yard. The engine had arrived. Would someone please come and get it? It turned out to weigh thirty tons. Without any way of transporting such a monster and with not nearly enough space to display or store it, the museum had to keep putting the Navy off. At this point several years have come and gone. The engine still is at the Navy yard. The Navy still wants to know when the museum is coming to get it. And the museum still is stymied.

RECONSTRUCTION AND RESTORATION
The growing number of outdoor museums acquire their most

[3] *Smithsonian Year 1965,* annual report of The Smithsonian Institution, pp. 118, 138; Karp, *The Smithsonian Institution,* pp. 82–3.

important possessions—their houses, shops, churches, and other buildings—in at least one of three ways. They restore old buildings already on their property. They find other old structures and move them to the museum. They construct new buildings using old buildings as models. At the Village Crossroads in Coopers-town, New York, all the buildings come from elsewhere. The smaller ones were moved lock, stock, and barrel to the museum. The larger ones were cut into sections, moved, then put back together again. Each building—there are twelve as I write this—dates from the first half of the nineteenth century and was pains-takingly searched out in the villages, towns, and hamlets of the area. The museum's church presented the biggest problem. It took the curators fifteen years to find the right one. Not only did it have to come from the right area and the right period in time, it had to look as if it belonged, which meant that the architectural style and the size of the building also had to be right. Over the years some ninety churches were considered. The one finally selected was found in Cornwallville only sixty-eight miles away.

The Shelburne Museum's many buildings near Shelburne, Ver-mont, including a lighthouse and a covered bridge, also were brought to the museum from elsewhere in the state, wherever Electra Havemeyer Webb, the museum's owner, happened to spot something she liked that was available. Her supreme achievement, however, was moving the sidewheeler *Ticonderoga* from Lake Champlain almost two miles overland to the museum. Here was another case where only a well-financed museum could function. Mrs. Webb's husband bought the boat for cash. But there re-mained the problem of getting it to Shelburne. It was, after all, 220 feet long and three decks high. As a first step, a huge basin was dug in Shelburne Bay. Then the boat was brought in by tugs and trapped with a construction of a huge clay dike behind it. Next, using a system of specially constructed locks, it was raised twenty-five feet onto a steel cradle which was supported by two flatcars, each on its own set of 400-foot-long tracks. When the flatcars reached the end of the tracks, they were brought to a halt, and the

As all the buildings at Village Crossroads in Cooperstown, New York, this church and this farmhouse and barn were moved to the museum from their original sites. *Courtesy New York State Historical Association*

trackage already covered was picked up and laid down again. Sixty-five days, twenty hours, and twenty-eight minutes were needed for the boat to make its last journey.[4]

The redevelopment of the mountaineer hamlet of Cades Cove near Townsend, Tennessee, in the heart of the Great Smoky Mountains is quite a different story. Since the early 1800's when German, Irish, Scotch, and English immigrants first settled what they called "Kate's Cove," the broad green valley has been a home to farmers. In fact, the valley still is farmed, in some cases by descendants of the original settlers. Moreover the pioneer buildings, restored by the National Park Service and the Great Smoky Mountain Natural History Association, are originals which stand today where they always have stood.

Although it also looks old, Old Sturbridge Village in Sturbridge, Massachusetts, is actually a creation of the imagination dating to 1936. No country village stood where it stands now. Almost all of its buildings either were moved to Sturbridge or reconstructed there with buildings elsewhere serving as models. Another stage set of this sort is Mystic Seaport in Mystic, Connecticut, built in the style of a nineteenth century New England waterfront village. In this case, however, all its buildings are modern structures.

The restoration of Colonial Williamsburg, on the other hand, is based on the most intensive archaeological research ever carried out in the United States. Some 244 sites have been explored as researchers have attempted to establish with certainty just what Williamsburg was like two centuries ago. In some cases the problem was restoring existing buildings to their original appearance. In others, it was reconstructing buildings of which no surface traces remained. To date some eighty-five buildings have been restored and fifty more have been rebuilt. One of the most recent reconstructions is the cabinetmaker's shop on Nicholson Street, which was owned first by Anthony Hay, then by Benjamin Buck-

[4] Saarinen, *The Proud Possessors*, pp. 302–3.

The cabinetmaking shop of Anthony Hay at Colonial Williamsburg in Virginia, reconstructed on the basis of archaeological and historical research. *Courtesy of Colonial Williamsburg*

trout, and finally by Edmund Dickinson. Archaeological evidence showed that the original shop was constructed sometime between 1745 and 1756. Maps, records, and archaeology show that the building was torn down sometime around 1780. In its day, furniture was made there, as were cradles, coffins, and harpsichord cases. Yet where the shop flourished in the mid-eighteenth century and a house stood and a kitchen and also a well, all that remained in mid-twentieth century was an empty lot bisected by a stream. Today the shop lives again. A master craftsman named John Heuvel, using the kinds of hand tools Hay used, turns out articles Colonial Williamsburg needs and others that visitors may buy. The Hay shop offers a good example of how a team of historians, archaeologists, architects, and experts in furnishings can re-create a building and a way of doing things that time has obliterated.

A first step in re-creating the shop was to know more of Anthony Hay and his life. The local newspaper was one source. It reported that Hay was living in Williamsburg by 1751; that in 1756 he purchased the Nicholson Street property from Thomas Everard, the clerk of York County; that in 1767 he borrowed 4,000 pounds, sold his shop to Mr. Bucktrout, and acquired the famous Raleigh Tavern. From Hay's diary it was learned that one of his patrons at the tavern was George Washington. From account books it was found that he ordered many magazines and books from England, as well as Latin, grammar, and spelling texts for his seven children. By tracing his family, it also was learned that one of his sons, George Hay, grew up to become the Federal attorney who prosecuted Aaron Burr for treason.

Another early step was exploratory excavation which confirmed, as records and maps already showed, that this indeed was the site. Full-scale work began in January, 1960, and continued for more than five years. The brick foundations the archaeologists first uncovered told a great deal about the shop: its dimensions, the size of the first floor, the type of basement it had, and the location and even the height of a flight of stairs. Differences in the age of the brick showed where an extension to the building had been constructed. The presence of clay fill showed that part of the shop had been constructed in the bed of a diverted stream. The remains of brick piers showed that part of the extension had been built over the stream's new bed.[5] Why the shop finally was dismantled was explained by the discovery that the diverted stream had filled with silt to such an extent that the water had backed up against the building. Wall plaster and fragments of timber unearthed showed that the building was of frame construction. Large deposits of

---

[5] At the time of excavation the stream was running in still a third bed it had carved for itself. It now has been returned to the bed it occupied under the extension.

plaster helped establish where the windows and doors had been, since it was through these openings that the refuse had to be thrown when the house was taken down. The clay tiles and wooden shingles archaeologists found gave a picture of what the roof was like. A series of post holes and fence parts showed where the fence was and what it had been made of. Moreover, root holes of eighteenth century trees were found and served as a guide in relandscaping the site.

During the three years of actual excavation more than sixty thousand objects and fragments of objects were unearthed, which told not only of the building but also of cabinetmaking and of everyday life in that period. One of the most important sources of these artifacts were six feet of moist silt deposited by the diverted stream. Had many of the wooden and leather objects involved fallen in drier ground, much of what was preserved might well have disintegrated. Still other sources of material were old trash pits and Hay's well. Thus the many tools archaeologists unearthed told something of the techniques of the eighteenth century cabinetmaker. Discovery of a partially completed table leg, a piece of wall paneling, the end of an oboe, furniture hardware, upholstery tacks, and countless other objects gave a picture of what was made. Fragments of pottery suggested the kinds of dishes used, and served as a guide in finding others like them for display. Sugar tongs, candleholders, teapots, and tankards told more of everyday life. So did a tin-plated cooking vessel from Hay's well which also solved a minor mystery. Up to that point, historians did not know how to distinguish between tinware made in the eighteenth century and that of the nineteenth century. The cooking vessel was found with other items known to have been made in the eighteenth century, indicating its age and thereby establishing the age of others like it. The artifacts uncovered at the Hay site and elsewhere in Colonial Williamsburg serve as furnishings, as displays, and also as impressive scholarly collections of eighteenth century life which are an important resource for researchers on the staff and elsewhere.

Archaeology also has been used in Independence National Historical Park in Philadelphia, although to a lesser extent. In addition to determining the appearance and construction of various buildings, it has yielded many interesting household articles, including eighteenth century toothbrushes, combs, and eyeglass frames. Pits that were attached to the privies then in use are a major source of such material, since it was common practice in Philadelphia in those days to use one's privy pit much as one uses a trashcan today.

Along with archaeology, museums also rely heavily on documents in restoring or reconstructing a building. The detailed surveys made by insurance companies in determining just what it is they are insuring and what rate to charge sometimes are an invaluable source of help. Of course so are plans and official records when they are available. In addition, prints, paintings, drawings, and cartoons may show what the outside or inside of a building looked like at a particular time. Newspaper accounts also may be useful. In the recent restoration of Independence Hall to its appearance between 1775 and 1800, officials at the National Historical Park actually have had a great deal to go on: the original elevation and floor plan done about the time the building was erected, account books of the government of Pennsylvania covering work done on the building in the eighteenth and nineteenth centuries, the records and photographs of a restoration undertaken in the 1890's when some original portions of the building were removed, and many prints and paintings. However, it will have far less to go on in its reconstruction of City Tavern, the building where the Continental Congress first met in 1774. Even the foundations have been destroyed. At this point the principal clues lie in insurance surveys and a few early prints.

On the other hand, curators at George Washington's Mount Vernon estate in Virginia were absolutely clear on the kind of shingles they would need to reroof the many buildings there. They even knew the color that the shingles originally had been painted. The problem was finding the kind of wood with which

Restoration of the house where Dolley Todd lived in Philadelphia before she married James Madison. *Courtesy Independence National Historical Park*

they had been made—it was virgin swamp cypress of which there was very little remaining—and then finding a few of the vanishing breed of men who knew how to split shingles by hand in the way it was done two centuries ago. After a long search a few remaining stands of cypress were found between Williamsburg and Richmond on the banks of the Pamunket River. By asking and asking, the shinglemakers were also finally tracked down.

Finding the original furnishings of historic buildings is often even more difficult. In the case of Independence Hall, however, and also Congress Hall some of the originals are on hand. In Independence Hall the chair from which Washington presided over the Continental Congress in 1787 is in place, as is the inkstand that was used eleven years earlier by the men who signed the Declaration of Independence. Next door, in the Senate Chamber in Congress Hall, twenty-three of the chairs and two of the desks that the first United States Senators used, when Philadelphia was the nation's capital from 1790 to 1800, also are in place. Here identification was easy. Washington's chair was made in 1778 for the speaker of the Pennsylvania Assembly which then met in

The only original objects in the Assembly Room at Independence Hall are at the back of the room, the chair which George Washington used at the Continental Congress in 1787 and, on the table in front of it, the inkstand used when the Declaration of Independence was signed. *Courtesy Independence National Historical Park*

Independence Hall. It has never strayed from government hands. The same is true of the inkstand and of the chairs and desks in the Senate chamber.

When it is impossible to obtain the originals, antiques believed to be like the originals are sought. When antiques are not available, modern reproductions are used. Although there are twenty-three of the original chairs in the Senate chamber, the remaining ten are missing and reproductions are used in their place. In this instance, the government knows who owns some of the missing originals and has hopes of obtaining them. On the other hand, the desks and chairs in Independence Hall are reproductions of what curators think they were like, based on existing evidence. If better evidence indicates that the furniture was different, then new reproductions would be made.

Does it matter that often originals are not used? Some curators contend that it does. They say that the experience of seeing a room as it actually was means far more to a visitor and has a greater emotional impact on him than when antiques from the period or reproductions are used. Other curators I have talked with disagree. They say that original objects really aren't that important in an exhibit, that what counts is the overall impression that is made.

In refurnishing the private homes preserved in Independence National Historical Park, the curators rely heavily on inventories of estates and on letters and other personal papers to learn what inhabitants of a house owned and used. When originals are not available, which generally is the case, they also try to obtain antiques and, failing that, seek reproductions. Deciding just where to place furnishings is another problem. Often it is a matter of relying solely on experience and intuition. In other cases, marks on floors and walls offer clues. The original color in which a room was painted also is a puzzle. The solution lies in delicately scraping through all the paint that has accumulated over the years—at times, six or more layers—until the two bottom layers are reached, then determining, based on one's experience and on history,

Mendel Peterson of the
Museum of History and
Technology in Washington
exploring a 16th century
vessel sunk in the waters
off Bermuda. He is setting
a measuring device over
the vessel's timbers.
*Courtesy The Smithsonian
Institution*

whether the first layer actually was the first one that showed or was
an undercoat. From that point, it is a matter of matching the
original color with a modern paint.

Some of the most exciting archaeological work by an American
museum is being carried out under water off the Bermuda coast by
Mendel L. Peterson of the Smithsonian's Museum of History and
Technology, the man who rescued all the dimestore glassware.
Using light diving gear, Mr. Peterson has explored over fifty
wrecks of warships and trading ships dating back to the sixteenth
century. His objective: to learn more about the development of
ships and their armament and other equipment, to find out more
about routes and cargoes in the Colonial trade, and to help
document the introduction of European culture into the New
World. Although dramatic discoveries rarely are forthcoming,
much is being learned. In exploring the French frigate *L'Her-
minie,* which sank in 1838, he recovered a firing mechanism for

heavy guns which may represent a landmark in the development of such equipment. On still older wrecks he has encountered a kind of ammunition that previously was unknown, a series of small lead balls the size of buckshot connected by wires which made the balls expand when they were fired.

One of the great advantages of underwater archaeology is that each wreck is what is known as "a closed site." Thus once it is determined when a wreck occurred, everything aboard automatically is dated. Moreover, one knows where all the artifacts came from, where they were going, and what relationship they had to one another. In recent years Peterson has made great strides in adapting the techniques of the land-bound archaeologist to his underwater searches. He has developed special measuring devices and photographic equipment to provide accurate data needed for the drawings and records so essential to such collecting. Since the ships Mr. Peterson explores lie in relatively shallow waters, he usually is not their first visitor and often much of value already has been salvaged. When more advanced diving gear enables the archaeologist to explore the deeper portions of the ocean, wrecks will become available which have been untouched since they sank hundreds of years ago, vessels that truly are time capsules.

EXHIBITS

One still finds many history museums that have cases filled with arrowheads, rooms filled with furniture, and other rooms jammed with farm equipment. Such displays can be rather pleasant in that they permit the visitor to do his own exploring and make his own discoveries. By looking closely and carefully at such exhibits there is quite a bit one can learn. On the other hand, a little is likely to go a long way and unless a visitor has a deep interest in arrowheads or chairs with rawhide bottoms or plows, the amount of material and the way in which it is displayed may teach him only that some museums are tedious places. As a result, more and more history museums have been displaying less and less, just as the art museums do. The difference is that while an art museum may display an object primarily for its own sake, a history museum uses its objects primarily to illustrate a story which will help people to better understand history. It was with this in mind that the Farmers' Museum in Cooperstown, New York, put 75 per cent of its plows, barrows, reapers, and churns into storage and replaced them with an exhibit called the Farmer's Year. The exhibit relates month by month the changing tasks and responsibilities of a farm family in upstate New York in the first half of the nineteenth century. A number of farm implements and tools are displayed, but the emphasis is on the people involved. In addition to the equipment, there are photographs, drawings, and printed explanations. In the section on the month of March, for example, under "sugaring off" the visitor learns:

One of the first signs of spring is the sap rising in the sugar maples, as a result of sunny days and clear nights. At this time the farmer would tap his trees. The sap was boiled down to a syrup, or reduced to a sugar. By this process, the farmer was able to obtain an extra cash crop, and satisfy the sweet-tooth of the nation.

To give a further sense of what was involved for a farm family, there are demonstrations of the skills they needed. Thus, local craftsmen make broom corn into brooms and others turn flax into linen. At the Oregon Historical Society in Portland only a small proportion of its objects is being used to tell the story of the state from prehistoric times through early settlement. As we shall see, the same approach is being applied in the Museum of History and Technology in Washington, D.C., to describe how the armed forces of the United States have developed.

The Settlement of New Amsterdam. Traditionally, history museums have organized their possessions in individual collections and have developed their exhibits in terms of those collections. For example, fire-fighting equipment and everything relating to fire-fighting usually is collected and exhibited together. This is also true of maritime equipment, furniture, silver, and so on.

At the Museum of the City of New York, for the purposes of

exhibits, these traditional boundaries have been eliminated. A series of galleries is being developed which will trace the history of the city of New York from the settlement of New Amsterdam to the present. The objective in each gallery is to offer a total picture of an era: the important events and personalities, the major political and economic problems, and the way in which the people lived in that period. The first in the series is the Dutch Gallery which takes a visitor from the scientific and historic events of the sixteenth century through the Age of Exploration to New Amsterdam and life there until the British arrived in 1664.

The material dealing with life in New Amsterdam is concerned with economic activity, home life, education, religion, and recreation. To tell this story, the museum is using objects from many of its collections. Where it didn't have what was needed, it borrowed material or had copies made. Thus the visitor finds early navigational instruments, early armaments, a Chinese porcelain dish of the sixteenth century, a tomahawk and a war club, a pair of silver saltcellars dated 1623, Dutch coins, a sword and spoon believed to be those Peter Stuyvesant used, and original furnishings used in New Amsterdam. The museum also had an imposing millstone it wanted to display, and therefore had a working model of a New Amsterdam mill built so that visitors would understand how such equipment operated. Using the original plans, it also had a section of a New Amsterdam house built. At the center of the gallery, workmen reproduced one of the bastions of Fort Orange, which was just below what is now Bowling Green at the foot of Manhattan Island. The fort is large enough to stand in. From the top of it there is an excellent view of a 360-degree painting of New Amsterdam which shows what one would have seen from the fort had he been standing there in 1660.

Visitors enter the gallery through a darkened passageway which is designed to help them make the transition from the twentieth century to the sixteenth. On the walls in fluorescent paint are illustrations and a brief text which tell of the events that prompted the Dutch to come to North America and settle on Manhattan Island.

Information on the economic life of New Amsterdam and the role of the local government was readily obtained from laws, decrees, account books, and business correspondence the museum had available. But the details of everyday life were more difficult to obtain since few diaries, journals, or other accounts had survived. The curators reasoned, however, that people from Holland would live in New Amsterdam as they did in their native country, only more simply. Using this approach, they turned to existing material on seventeenth century life in Holland and also to the folk art of the period, borrowing from other museums almost four hundred prints, drawings, etchings, and paintings which showed scenes from everyday life. As information was gathered, it was organized by category and listed on index cards. By the time the research was done, 1,300 cards bearing 130,000 words had been prepared. Assembling the gallery took the largest part of three

A workman at the Museum of the City of New York reconstructs part of a Dutch fort that stood in New Amsterdam in 1660. The painting above the fort depicts New Amsterdam as it appeared at that time. *Courtesy Museum of the City of New York: photograph, Alfred A. Kester*

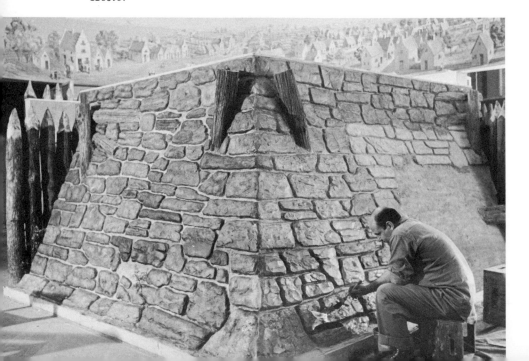

years. Almost everybody on the staff was involved: the director, the assistant director, the senior curator, the designer, the education staff, the publicity director, and all the painters, carpenters, and electricians.

A Trip Through Time. The Milwaukee Public Museum in Wisconsin also draws from its collections in many fields to prepare an individual gallery. In an imaginative gallery called "A Trip Through Time" the objective is to provide a brief chronological picture of the formation of the earth, the development of man, and the rise of civilization. The visitor starts by peering out at the earth as it might be seen through the portholes of a space ship five hundred miles from the moon. Then, as the map on page 153 shows, he walks along a winding corridor through exhibits that take him from earliest geologic time through the Age of Reptiles and the Age of Mammals to the caveman and the Bronze Age. From that point exhibits deal with the rise of civilization in Egypt, Greece, and Rome and the development of religion, communica-

Plan of a gallery at the Milwaukee Public Museum which draws on the museum's collections in natural history, history, and art in telling the story of man's development. Most museums build exhibits around individual collections. *Courtesy Milwaukee Public Museum*

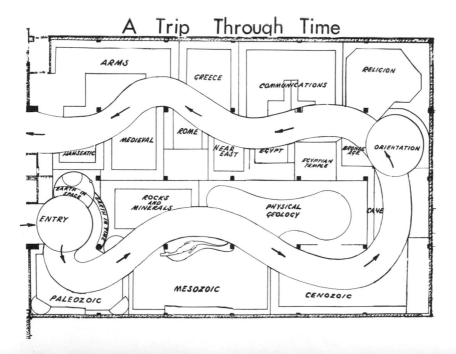

tions, and arms. Finally, the visitor enters the Middle Ages and the Age of Exploration. From there he crosses a broad lobby—perhaps the Atlantic Ocean—to the New World which, in this case, happens to be Wisconsin and the re-created streets of Old Milwaukee.

The Shoemaker's Story. At the Roberson Memorial Center in Binghamton, New York, which has few collections of its own, an exhibit may grow into a cultural happening. Take, for example, "The Shoemaker's Story," an exhibit all about shoes which was of considerable interest in an area where one of the biggest industries is shoemaking. From the Medical Center of the University of Rochester came a display on the human foot and what it needs in the way of footwear. From the local World Affairs Council came an exhibit on the international sources of raw materials without which shoes could not be produced in the United States. From the shoe manufacturers came the materials themselves, as well as shoe machinery and examples of shoes used in various occupations and activities. From that source also came the equipment for a one-man shoemaking shop a craftsman operated. From many sources came examples of footwear which illustrated the history of shoes around the world, from the feather "shoes" of the Australian bushman to the sandals of the early Roman. These were displayed with paintings, costumes, and other materials which depicted life in the areas and periods involved. From the United States Army came an exhibit of military footwear. A display on the role of the shoe in mythology and fairy tales also was developed. Moreover, the local Musical Arts Society created a ballet program which showed how, in fashioning ballet slippers, the shoemaker affects ballet and its music.

Socialites and Immigrants. The exhibit focusing on a single incident or event also can be highly effective. One involving socialites was developed by the Chicago Historical Society. It concerned the gowns worn by those Chicago women who were presented to the king and queen of England in the period from 1900 to 1932. The dresses displayed were all in the museum's collections, such as the one worn by Catherine Hatton Crerar in 1925, a "straight, beltless, knee-length gown of iridescent sequins on pink chiffon over pink silk" with a matching court train. However, there was research to be done on the presentations themselves and on the women involved. In addition, the gowns had to be cleaned, repaired, and fitted on mannequins; accessories such as fans, veils, bags, and gloves had to be selected; props had to be designed and made; and labels had to be written, printed, and mounted.

The immigrants who came to New York from 1870 to 1924 and settled in Manhattan on the Lower East Side were recalled in an exhibit prepared by the Jewish Museum in New York. The exhibit's big feature was 150 blow-ups of photographs on what things were like. Sewing machines and other equipment from garment factories where so many immigrants had jobs also were displayed, as were paintings and drawings of the Lower East Side. Two films were shown continuously, including one in which actor Zero Mostel reads letters written long ago to the *Jewish Daily Forward*. So popular was the exhibit, in its first seven weeks 80,000 people came to see it; then it went on the road to other museums that had requested it. Many of the visitors were immigrants themselves. For them, it was a nostalgic experience. As an older man staring at a photograph of newly arrived immigrants told a younger man at his side, "Louis, that could be me."[6]

Planning an Exhibit. No matter how simple or complex it may be, every exhibit is based on a plan. In many of the larger museums this involves preparing a script which describes in detail the theme to be covered and which objects, prints, photographs, and other visual materials are to be used. As with the Dutch Gallery, usually quite a bit of research is needed before a curator can complete his plan.

At the Smithsonian's Museum of History and Technology three curators spent a total of four months developing a script for the

[6] New York *Times,* September 21, 1966.

large permanent gallery devoted to the evolution of the armed forces in the United States. Based on their research, the curators prepared a detailed statement of the objectives of the gallery and all the headlines and labels to be used. The headlines were designed to tell at a glance the significance of the period represented. For example, instead of using "The Revolutionary War" as a headline, the curators decided on "The War for Independence" since it describes what the war and the period were all about; instead of "The War of 1812," they decided on "Defending Our Sovereignty." Such headings are the first level of information in an exhibit and may provide all a casual visitor wants to know. Two kinds of labels also were prepared. One type was designed for the person seeking only a small amount of information. These briefly described what happened and why. The other labels, for a visitor with a deeper interest, went into a subject in far more detail.

The Smithsonian is unusual in that it has an editor whose job it is to review all scripts and make the headlines and labels read as smoothly as possible. One copy of the script went to him. Others went to the artist who would work with the curators in designing the exhibit and to the production staff whose job it would be to build the exhibit and install it. Throughout, an advisory committee of historians and other experts on the subject also were involved, reacting to the curators' plans, reviewing their material, and making suggestions relating to accuracy and approach.

In all, about two years were needed to develop and install the gallery. The cost was roughly $200,000, which covered all materials, special display cases, the development of highly intricate ship models, and the purchase of original objects that the museum did not have in its collections.

Of course, few museums have that much money or time to spend on exhibits. A display prepared by the Minnesota Historical Society on the history of newspapers in its state is perhaps more typical. It was planned, prepared, and installed in about two months at a cost of under $1,000. Ordinarily exhibit budgets for an entire year may come to but a few thousand dollars. When this

A portion of one of the re-created streets of Old Detroit at the Detroit Historical Museum.
Courtesy Detroit Historical Museum

is taken into account, it is remarkable that some history museums are able to produce the kinds of exhibits they do.

EXHIBITING TECHNIQUES

The Streets of Old Detroit. In the basement of the Detroit Historical Museum there is a street along which one can stroll which re-creates the city as it was in 1840; nearby there is another which shows what things were like thirty years later in 1870. Material is now being gathered for two more such streets, one for the year 1900, and another for the year 1930. The streets already in existence have sidewalks, roadways, storefronts and interiors, street lamps, horse troughs, trees, and even a firehouse with a fireman's pole that has been greased to keep visitors from climbing it. The storefronts are a byproduct of urban renewal.

Whenever the city tears down an old neighborhood which has buildings that may be useful to the museum, somebody calls up Dan Kinsler, the museum's chief exhibits specialist, and he rushes out to take a look. If he sees something he can use, he calls for a salvage crew. The storefronts for the 1840 street were obtained when the city was replacing its riverfront area; those from the 1870 street are from the section that was torn up for the John C. Lodge Freeway.

But finding the storefronts is only part of the job. A street is a complicated affair, even if, like those in the museum, it is but sixty or seventy feet long. For example, since wooden storefronts in Detroit of the 1840's were not painted, the paint which had been added to those the museum acquired had to be stripped off. Moreover, the newly stripped wood had to look weathered and dirty. To achieve in minutes what it took the elements years to do, Mr. Kinsler painted the wood with a thin turpentine to which a small amount of white pigment had been added. Often new window glass also had to be installed. To make it look old, one side was coated with lacquer. As the lacquer dried, an exhibit man blew a stream of air on it with a compressor, which gave the glass a wavy quality such as it would have had if manufactured a century or more ago.

What kinds of stores the old storefronts enclosed originally have little to do with the stores behind them now. In every case, however, the stores re-created are stocked and furnished as they would have been in the 1840's and 1870's. In the General Store even the smells are as they should be. But on the day it was to be dedicated, alas, this wasn't the case. Instead of the enticing odors of spices, cheese, and tobacco, it smelled of fresh paint. To replace the smell with a more appropriate one, the ever-resourceful Mr. Kinsler spent several hours over a hot plate, brewing a can of water loaded with spices. By the time the dedication ceremony began, everything smelled as it should.

The contents of the stores all came from the museum's collections; the lettering on the windows and signs also is authentic. To give the streets a varied appearance, stone and brick storefronts have been included with the wooden ones, though the bricks and the stones are necessarily copies. The brick is made of plaster, the stone of papier-mâché. The slate sidewalks are real, however, and so are the pavements: the cobblestones in the 1840 street and the round cedar blocks in the 1870 streets. The old-fashioned lamp-posts are also authentic, but the lighting fixtures they support were harder to come by. The museum could find only one. The others it uses are copies, fashioned in its shop from old tin cans. A genuine Wells Fargo safe for the local bank was also impossible to

obtain; so Mr. Kinsler and his staff created one out of papier-
mâché and plaster which is so realistic-looking it would fool a
safecracker. A hitching post also was needed, but wasn't available.
A new post was made with 4 by 4's, then it was aged with an acety-
lene torch and a vigorous wire brush scrubbing to give it the look
of authenticity. The pillars that hold up the ceiling above the
streets also were a problem in that they spoiled the effect. Since
there was no way to get rid of them, Mr. Kinsler turned them into
trees.

People Out of the Past.   Going even further in quest of reality,
the curators of the nation's outdoor museums often populate them
with people in costumes. Colonial Williamsburg goes to the
greatest lengths. Hundreds of its employees—guides, interpreters,
workmen, craftsmen, waiters and waitresses—spend their working
days in eighteenth century dress cut according to a tailor's manual
of the period. The craftsmen are among the most interesting. As
we have seen, there is a cabinetmaker. But there also are a wig-
maker, a clockmaker, a silversmith, a bookbinder, an engraver, a
milliner, a gunsmith, a bootmaker, a baker, and a printer. All
work in operating craft shops using eighteenth century tools to
create articles Williamsburg uses and visitors buy. There also is a
fifes and drums corps made up of nine fifers and nine drummers,
all local high school boys. When the militia parades during the
visitor season, they provide the music. The instruments they use
are wooden fifes, rope-tensioned drums, and two bass drums dating from the eighteenth century. There also is a junior fifes and
drums corps where younger boys train for vacancies that occur
when the older ones graduate from high school.

Old Sturbridge Village in Massachusetts, Greenfield Village in
Michigan, Mystic Seaport in Connecticut, and the Village Crossroads in New York also are inhabited during visiting hours. At
Village Crossroads a storekeeper sells tobacco, soap, candy and
such; a printer sets and prints a newspaper; a blacksmith pursues
his craft and a country doctor his. At the foot of the lane along
which the village is strung is Lippitt Farmhouse where two

Fifes and drums corps *(above)*, and craftsmen at the reconstructed
Anthony Hay cabinetmaking shop, both at Colonial Williamsburg.
Courtesy Colonial Williamsburg

women bake bread and cakes in a beehive oven, make cheese and butter, and dip candles. If you come along at the right time, they will offer you something to eat. Outside, farmhands tend to their chores, caring for livestock and raising crops. All are local residents, usually retired people. In this museum, however, the workers wear contemporary clothes. Only the women in the farmhouse are costumed. They say they feel more at home dressed that way.

Wax People. The so-called wax museums also are populated with people, but here the people are wax or plastic. One finds wax museums in such places as Washington, D.C.; New York; Philadelphia; Gettysburg; Harpers Ferry; Gatlinburg, Tennessee; Denver; Montreal; and Quebec. In all, there are over twenty-five. Aside from making as much money as possible, their objective is to dramatize important men and historic events through realistic life-size settings. Many of these museums have a particular theme. In Washington, D.C., the theme is memorable moments in American history, from the arrival of Leif Ericson to the assassination of John F. Kennedy and the election of Lyndon Johnson. En route one visits eighty settings inhabited by over two hundred plastic figures depicting such events as the arrival of Columbus, Pocahontas saving John Smith's life, the Salem witch trials, the signing of the Declaration of Independence, Davy Crockett fighting at the Alamo, President Cleveland getting married, and General MacArthur returning to the Philippine Islands. At Harpers Ferry, the emphasis is on John Brown; at Gettysburg it is on the battle; in Denver it is on the history of the West.

Many of the figures at the museum in Washington, D.C. are strikingly realistic. However, President Kennedy has been a problem. A number of efforts have been made to achieve a close likeness, but none has succeeded very well. All the figures are based on research to a greater or lesser degree. Living persons who have been selected for enshrinement are asked to fill out a form which provides data on their dimensions, age, complexion, hair color, eye color, and suit or dress size. They also are asked to provide photographs. Some go to great lengths to be helpful. Astronaut John Glenn, for example, yielded a lock of his hair to assure that the hair on his mannequin would be just the right shade. To get the information needed on Henry Ford's appearance, a copy of his 1916 Michigan driver's license was obtained. To get Babe Ruth's height and weight, the same approach was used. To get the pockmarks on Washington's face just right, eighteenth century treatments of smallpox were studied. Of course the farther back in history one goes, the less there is to rely on regarding how individuals looked. Pocahontas, for example, was a girl of fourteen when she pleaded for John Smith's life, but all researchers could find were illustrations which showed her as a mature woman. As a result, Pocahontas in plastic is a combination of many pleasant-looking Indian maidens. Davy Crockett was an-

Pocahontas pleads with her father Powhatan to save John Smith's life, one of the scenes depicted at the National Historical Wax Museum in Washington, D.C. As Smith awaits his fate, his chest moves up and down as he "breathes" with the aid of an electric pump. *Courtesy National Historical Wax Museum*

other problem of this sort. In the end he came out looking like an angry version of Fess Parker, who then was TV's Davy Crockett.

Animation is playing a growing role in the wax museums. In Washington, for example, John Smith's chest heaves as Pocahontas saves his life, Mark Twain rocks in a rocking chair, Columbus's boat also rocks, lightning flashes as Franklin flies his kite, coffee bubbles as Lincoln talks with his generals, and Harry Truman plays the "Missouri Waltz." The figures at the Washington wax museum and its half-dozen affiliated museums are made in Baltimore at the Lynch Display Corporation, which is headed by a former window trimmer and mannequin repairman named Earl Dorfman. Heads, hands, and anything else that shows are sculptured in clay, then cast in a lifelike plastic. The rest of a figure usually is wood. The costumes come from a theatrical supply house and the props for the settings from many places. The cost of a costumed figure ranges from $1,000 to about $1,500. Should you be curious as to who Mr. Dorfman is, look for the mannequin of the sleeping workman at the Museum of Famous People in New York and also at the National Historical Wax Museum in Washington. In both places it is his face you will be looking at.

Sound and Light. The sound-and-light presentation is still another approach the commercial historian uses in dramatizing history. On an enormous electric map at the Musée du Fort in Quebec, colored lights and gun flashes re-create the many battles in the city's history as a narrator tells of the stirring events. At Stone Mountain Memorial Park outside Atlanta a similar approach is used in recounting General Sherman's march to the sea during the Civil War. At the Heritage Center in Boston the subject is the events that led to the American Revolution. The techniques used include simultaneous life-size projections from a half-dozen sources, color, and stereophonic sound.

EDUCATION
The audience is school children, the objective to provide a tour or a lesson which makes what is learned in the classroom more

meaningful. At the Milwaukee Public Museum four registered teachers work with school groups from throughout the city, offering carefully planned lessons in which museum objects are used to give a sense of life in Colonial times. Visiting youngsters may fire an unloaded musket in which the flint creates a shower of sparks, operate a churn, put bread in a beehive oven, write with a quill pen, dip candles, and spin linen. At the Museum of the City of New York there are the famed "Please Touch" exhibits on Dutch life in early New York which enable youngsters to handle things used in those days: wooden shoes, a churn, a cradle, old-fashioned ice skates, a leather fire bucket, pewter plates, a beautiful brass milk jug, a foot warmer, and other things as well. Alas, the wooden shoes may not be tried. One is likely to pick up splinters unless he is wearing socks as thick as those the Dutch wore. In a recent year some seventy thousand school children came to visit the museum. There was neither room nor time for any more. By early November, in fact, all the school tours through the following June had been spoken for. Although seventy thousand school children may seem like a great many, in a city like New York ten times that number could benefit. Several such museums are clearly needed. In other cities the problem is not a great deal different.

Other teaching methods also are used. At the Seattle Museum of History and Industry collections of early tools, clothing, and toys are sent to the schools for teachers to explain and children to examine. In Detroit the Dossin Great Lakes Museum loans teachers navigational instruments and other maritime equipment for classroom use. At the Milwaukee Public Museum four truckloads of film, filmstrips, and displays on history, and also natural history and art, are dispatched each week to 328 schools in the city and its suburbs. From the State Historical Society of Wisconsin in Madison, a history museum on wheels each year carries the story of the state to upwards of a hundred cities and towns. At Colonial Williamsburg each year, under the Student Burgesses program, high school students gather from all over the United States and from many foreign countries for discussion meetings on such important issues as individual freedom and the right and responsibility to protest. In a totally different kind of effort Mystic Seaport operates the Mystic Mariner Training Program which gives youngsters from fourteen to eighteen experience in seamanship and sailing. Participants live aboard the 118-foot square-rigger *Joseph Conrad* and learn to sail small craft on Connecticut's Mystic River. Advanced students get a taste of seagoing life through week-long training cruises as members of the crew of the schooner *Brilliant*.

Relatively few history museums, however, offer programs for adults. Of these, one of the most pleasant are the walking tours that Henry Hope Reed, Jr., conducts for the Museum of the City of New York through the city's diverse neighborhoods. There is even such a tour for young people, a guide to "George Washington's New York."

A group of New Yorkers visit Plymouth Church in Brooklyn on a Sunday morning walking tour sponsored by the Museum of the City of New York. *Courtesy Museum of the City of New York: photograph, Alfred A. Kester*

RESEARCH

The museum historian's quest for knowledge takes many forms. As we have seen, it may involve archaeology or a search for artifacts or documents or reading or talking with people either to obtain objects that are needed or to be sure that exhibits are authentic. At times, however, the research has little to do with exhibits as such. Instead it may involve how one can restore a priceless, historic photograph that has faded from sight, or what the origins of an old plow are, or what it was like to be a sailor on a merchant ship at the turn of the century, or what kinds of musical instruments are being played in the mountainous back country of North Carolina or what techniques were used in drilling the first commercial American oil well.

The restoration of images on old photographs, as shown on page 167, was an achievement of Eugene Ostroff, associate curator of photography at the Museum of History and Technology in Washington. The photographs involved were well over a century old. With their images gone, they were useless for research or display. The method Mr. Ostroff developed to restore them was as follows: A faded print first was treated with neutrons in an atomic reactor, with the result that some of its image silver was converted to radioactive isotopes. Then the print was placed in contact for a short period with an unexposed sheet of X-ray film. When the X-ray film was processed, an image appeared like the one originally on the print.

The origins of the old plow were uncovered at the Farmers' Museum in Cooperstown, New York, as part of the continuing research all history museums try to conduct on those objects they own that they don't know enough about. The plow was a one-wheel hand type. When one of the curators spotted it among the dozens of plows in the museum, its appearance told him it was something special. Research among illustrations of early plows finally identified it as an eighteenth century German plow, a finding that visiting European curators later confirmed. How did it

Top: Photograph of a table setting made about 1841 by W.H.F. Talbot, an Englishman who invented the photographic negative. Bottom: The same photograph restored through research at the Museum of History and Technology in Washington, D.C. *Courtesy The Smithsonian Institution*

get to upstate New York? Germans had settled north and east of Cooperstown. In all likelihood they either brought it with them or copied it from those they knew in their native land.

A museum historian concerned with what a sailor's life was like is Harlan Soeten, curator at the San Francisco Maritime Museum. For a number of years he has been tape-recording interviews with old seamen to find out about their experiences aboard the sailing ships that once moved in and out of San Francisco Bay. Most of those still alive are in their eighties and nineties and do not have many more years. The stories of their experiences, if not recorded, will die with them. One man, whose experiences are now preserved as history, went whaling with hand harpoons in an old bark out of Boston Harbor in 1912. Still another, a San Franciscan of ninety-four, recalls the days when men in San Francisco who had no interest in going to sea were shanghaied and went against their wills. To guard against exaggerated sea stories, Mr. Soeten closely questions his subjects on specific points, then checks answers that seem doubtful against existing records and with other seamen. As funds are available, the hundreds of tapes he has recorded are slowly being transcribed.

The Museum of History and Technology in Washington, D.C., is another museum that uses the technique of oral history. Last year C. Malcolm Watkins, curator of social history, journeyed to Moore County, North Carolina, to learn from the people who live there how they make their pottery and how their parents and grandparents made theirs. In another project in North Carolina, and also in Virginia, recordings were made of folk songs mountain people sing and of the handmade dulcimers and banjos they use to accompany themselves. How were the instruments made? Were they always made that way? The answers also were recorded and now are part of history.

Research on methods used to drill the first commercial oil well in the United States was another recent Smithsonian project, as was research on bark canoes and skin boats of North America, electromagnetic instruments, and one of the oldest screw-cutting machines in existence.

Of what use is all this knowledge? What meaning does it have in modern life? Frank Taylor, director of the United States National Museum—which includes the Museum of History and Technology and the Museum of Natural History—suggests it is enough just to know. If knowledge has immediate practical application so much the better, but if this were the only reason for learning, he points out, man would not know a great deal. Yet the knowledge in good history museums does provide a framework for the solution of many modern problems. Certainly, if heeded, it can keep people from making the same mistakes over and over again. It also is a fruitful source of ideas. The old hot-air engines at the Museum of History and Technology are but one example. In the early days of the nineteenth century such engines were in common use on American farms in pumping water and performing other chores. They were small, simple, and safe and were fueled free of charge with corn cobs and wood scraps. Because they could not produce enough horsepower, however, eventually they were abandoned. In the late 1940's Mr. Taylor described these engines in a museum catalog, with the result that two engineers from Philips, the big Dutch industrial concern, spent several days in Washington studying them for a similar engine they were developing. A few years later the Army examined them in connection with a unit it needed that would provide heat and power for temporary quarters in cold climates. More recently the Navy became interested. They needed a simple, trouble-free engine for pumping oil through pipelines, and a modern hot-air engine could well be the answer.

VISITING A HISTORY MUSEUM

G. Carroll Lindsay of the Smithsonian Institution once said that to understand history one must know "what was sat upon, eaten from, ridden on, and lived in and with."[7] It is good advice for a

7 Katz, *Museums, U.S.A.*, p. 177.

visitor to a history museum. Only by taking into account that people as well as events were involved, people who really were not very different from people today, and by contrasting one's own life with theirs can he begin to appreciate what things were like. There also are other approaches which can make a visit more fruitful. One is to stop and read the sign in front of the museum so that you know what the museum's objective is. At the Farmers' Museum and Village Crossroads in Cooperstown, New York, the sign says that these museums "show how the plain people of yesterday, in doing their daily work, built a great nation, where only a great forest had stood." Down at Colonial Williamsburg the "sign" happens to be an elaborate million-dollar reception center where a film is shown that tells about Williamsburg and its restoration.

In some museums the "sign" may be a booklet. In others there may be no sign and it may be necessary to ask a member of the staff about the museum. In any case, it makes sense to know what you are going to look at before you begin. It also is useful to find out how a history museum is organized so that you can see it in the most effective way. Most are arranged either in the order in which the events they deal with occurred or by subject.

As far as the objects displayed are concerned, consider them on two levels: in terms of their design, craftsmanship, and detail and also in terms of their historical meaning. A tomahawk on display at the Oregon Historical Society is beautiful in its own right, but it also is believed to be the weapon used in 1847 to kill Dr. Marcus Whitman, a famous Indian missionary. The ship models on display at the Museum of History and Technology are another example. They are interesting for their own sakes, but they become even more so when one recognizes that the differences in their construction tell us something of the waters in which they had to operate and the trade in which they were engaged.

Attention to details, relationships, and meanings also is helpful in examining dioramas, the representations in miniature of important events and scenes. From the diorama of the New York City waterfront scene of the 1850's, shown on page 171, one can learn a great many things. The overall importance of clipper ships in the city's economy is illustrated. The primitive methods of loading, the complicated rigging, and the intricate decorations on the bows of the ships also are shown. The presence of an Oriental in native dress and, in a period well before the Civil War, of a Negro workman is of interest. So are the policeman's uniform and the way the women, merchants, sailors, and laborers are dressed, and the many different kinds of hats. Of possible interest to New Yorkers is the fact that many waterfront buildings like the ones shown are still in use.

Historic Houses. Since there is no better place to learn about someone than in his home, in visiting historic houses it is always fascinating to look for indications of what the owners were like. In its order and dignity, Mount Vernon reflects the deep influence of George Washington. In the many inventions and innovations at Monticello, Thomas Jefferson's estate at Charlottesville, Virginia, one clearly sees Jefferson's influence. In both cases what was at

Diorama of South Street on the New York City waterfront in 1850. *Courtesy Museum of the City of New York*

Top: A painting of George Washington's estate at Mount Vernon, Virginia as it appeared in his day. Bottom: The main house as it appears today. The shutters were added after the painting was done. *Courtesy Mount Vernon Ladies' Association*

work were the same creative energies they contributed to the development of their country. Of course, one also might approach such houses for their architecture, or their interior decoration or, as visitors are encouraged to do at Mount Vernon, as shrines.

Outdoor Museums. In visiting a restored or a reconstructed village, it is important to keep things in perspective. There is a tendency in such places to present the past as grander and more charming than it was. In fact, some of the outdoor museums have the look of today's prosperous suburbs, which is hardly what eighteenth-century towns were like. Lacking paint, pavement, and sewers, many were dusty, dirty, and rundown, and often smelly, as well.[8] The clothing used by those who "live" in these towns also may be somewhat misleading. Although the costumes themselves are likely to be authentic enough, they may not be what people wore most of the time. Some workmen in Colonial Williamsburg dress in their Sunday best the week around. In addition, as has been noted, such places weren't as much fun to live in as they are for a modern-day tourist to visit. On the other hand, they can be highly instructive. What seems most effective is trying to think of yourself not as a visitor from another culture and another time but as someone who actually lives there. One good way to make the transformation is to sit quietly on the lawn or walk about for a while without going into any of the buildings until you feel somewhat more at home.[9] The best time to visit an outdoor museum is the spring or fall when few other visitors are about. It was on such a day in early November, crisp enough for fires to have been lighted, that I walked virtually alone except for the "inhabitants" through the Village Crossroads in Cooperstown and came closer than I had ever before to making contact with the past.

[8] David Lowenthal, "The American Way of History," Columbia University *Forum,* Summer, 1966.
[9] George R. Clay, *The Lightbulb Angel,* New York State Historical Association, 1963.

4 | Natural History Museums

MEXICO'S BAJA CALIFORNIA IS A DESOLATE PENINSULA OF RUGGED mountains and bleached deserts extending south from American California for 760 miles. For most of its length it is no more than fifty miles wide; in some sections it is but twenty-five miles across. To the west is the Pacific. To the east is the Gulf of California, an arm of the Pacific known also as the Sea of Cortez. Still farther east is the Mexican mainland. Much of Baja California, the Sea of Cortez, and the many arid islands offshore are poorly known. In fact, some of the area has yet to be explored. Over the years, however, naturalists have been fascinated by what they have learned of Baja's mammals, birds, reptiles, plants and marine life.

Biologists from the California Academy of Sciences in San Francisco have explored the area repeatedly since 1888. Scientists from the San Diego Natural History Museum and from other institutions have also journeyed to Baja. Their objectives have been to learn as much about the plant and animal life as possible and to collect specimens for further study and for display. Academy scientists alone have published over 3,500 pages of scientific findings on the area. Yet there is much still to be learned if the picture is to be complete.

In June, 1964, a team of eleven scientists made the journey once again. This was to be a short trip of but two weeks. The focus was a chain of desert islands at the southern end of the Sea of Cortez extending, as indicated on the map below, in an irregular line from Loreto to La Paz. Of the eleven researchers, six came from the California Academy of Sciences staff, three from the San Diego Natural History Museum, one from the Mexican Institute of Biology, and one from the Belvediere Scientific Fund, which was helping to pay for the expedition. The scientists involved were

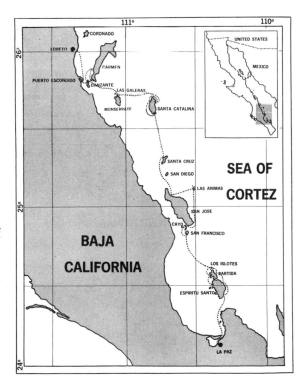

Route of the Sea of
Cortez Expedition.
*Courtesy California
Academy of Sciences:
map, Bob Olson*

The houseboat and the launch used on the Sea of Cortez Expedition.
Courtesy California Academy of Sciences: photograph, Robert T. Orr

experts on mammals, birds, scorpions, spiders, marine life, and plants. Two students accompanied the expedition, as did an underwater photographer and two television specialists from the Academy staff who were to make a film of the journey for use on a TV show. Members of the expedition flew from Tijuana just below San Diego to Loreto 575 miles to the south. Then they traveled by taxi to the nearby town of Puerto Escondido where a sixty-foot houseboat and a thirty-six-foot launch they were to use were waiting. Their boats carried them south from one island to the next. At each place, those with "land" interests remained ashore, while those with marine interests donned scuba gear to explore the surrounding waters. Each scientist collected specimens in his field, made observations, and recorded anything he saw of interest. Whatever was collected was then prepared, preserved, and packed for the journey home.

A detailed log kept by the Academy's director, George E. Lindsay, gives a picture of what the expedition was like. Here are some excerpts.[1]

[1] *Proceedings of the California Academy of Sciences.* Vol. XXX, No. 11 (December 31, 1964), pp. 211–42.

June 21   Puerto Escondido to Isla Danzante.

. . . Isla Danzante is a rough little island, only three and a half miles long and less than 500 feet high, and from the air it looks like a giant lizard. It was dry and land collecting was poor. Orr, Banks, and Bandar trapped but caught only six spiny pocket mice, *Perognathus spinatus seorsus*. Parrish, Muñoz, Marquardt, Sloan, and Lindsay collected after dark, finding only two scorpions, *Centruroides exilicauda*, some grasshoppers, camel crickets, and tubercular geckos. While waiting to be picked up on the beach we found isopods abundant and easy to capture, and bottled a large series of *Ligyda occidentalis*. No snakes have been reported from Isla Danzante, but Bandar found a fragment of a shed skin of a large snake while setting his traps. It was not collected at the time and he was unable to locate it the next day. . . .

June 23.   Isla Carmen to Las Galeras and Isla Monserrate.

. . . Some of the divers worked the depths as two-man teams while others explored the fissures in the barely submerged rocks with only snorkel equipment. It was a fantastic place. . . .

June 25.   Isla Santa Catalina.

Sloan collected five additional "rattleless rattlesnakes"! The first was found by Banks, coiled next to one of his mousetraps. . . . Sloan saw the second one under a *Pithecellobium* bush, and he then collected three more in a pile of brush under a large *Bursera* tree. . . . Lindsay picked up a second specimen of *Hypsiglena*. Three shed skins of *Crotalus catalinensis* were found under one bush. Sloan and Wiggins collected a long series of a live, endemic land snail, *Bulimulus johnstonii*, which was abundant under loose rocks and on the underside of logs. . . . This was a prolific spot for large fishes—amber jack, yellow tail, groupers to 300 pounds, golden cabrillo, and many others. Near the rocks there were many species of reef fish, parrot fish, wrasses, and others. In the bottom at intermediate depths were "forests" of burrowing eels which live in holes in the sand with only their heads and a few inches of their bodies exposed—all looking in the same direction. As a diver approached they sank out of sight, to reappear as soon as he passed. All attempts to anesthetize or dig out specimens were unsuccessful. The same experience was encountered later at Cabo San Lucas, and the reason is that this eel, whose exact identity is unknown at the moment, undoubtedly belongs to the pointed-tail ophichthid family, most of whose members can swim faster backwards in the sand than we less well-endowed human beings can swim forwards. . . . The Aquarium staff is currently working on an eel-dredge that will sneak up on these wary beasts faster than any skindiver; so if all goes well, Steinhart [the Academy's aquarium] will eventually have this elusive eel on display for the first time. . . .

June 26.   Isla Santa Catalina to Isla Santa Cruz and Isla San Jose.

. . . Parrish and Sloan captured two specimens of *Crotalus ruber* at the edge of a broad sandy arroyo which ran inland from the beach. Bandar captured one of *Crotalus mitchelli,* and Lindsay took a leafnose snake, *Phyllorhynchus decurtatus,* for an island record. Wiggins followed a fresh snake track to find a freshly dead example of the endemic brushrabbit, *Sylvilagus mansuetus,* which the reptile had apparently killed and was unable to swallow. The rabbit's skull was preserved, and additional specimens were taken. At dusk two bats, *Pipistrellus hesperus,* were shot by Orr and Parrish. Bandar spent the night on shore. . . .

June 29.   La Paz to Isla Partida.

We departed La Paz at 0200. The wind was up and the seas were rough, so we cruised up the sheltered east side of Isla Espiritu Santo and Isla Partida, to round the north end and anchor at 0615. Bandar came aboard with six mice, *Perognathus* and *Peromyscus,* three of which he caught in a single trap beside his sleeping bag. Orr was taken to Los Islotes, three rocky islets about one-half mile off the northern end of Isla Partida, to study the colony of sea lions there. Wiggins, Banks, and Parrish climbed an arroyo on Isla Partida to a large dry lake which was bordered with cliffs and *Ficus palmeri, Forchammeria watsonii,* and *Lysiloma candida.* They shot a "black" jack rabbit, *Lepus insularis,* for which Islas Partida and adjacent Espiritu Santo are famous among mammalogists. Most of the biologists did marine collecting or underwater photography. . . .

By July 3 the team had worked its way south to La Paz from where it flew back to the United States. What was accomplished? Here are some examples. On Isla Catalina they collected the rare "rattleless" rattlesnake, *Crotalus catalinensis,* which is known to live only on that barren island. Only four specimens had been collected previously. The scientists collected nine more, some of which can be seen at the Academy of Sciences and at the San Diego Zoo. They also answered a puzzling question regarding the sea lions in the Sea of Cortez. It had been thought for some time that there were no breeding grounds in the area and that the sea lions found there came in from the ocean. The discovery of a breeding ground on Los Islotes changed that assumption. In addition, they encountered a unique black jack rabbit which seemed to be limited to two small adjacent islands, Partida and Espiritu Santos. They increased their knowledge of the habits of the fish-eating bat which lives only in the area of the Sea of Cortez. They learned more about the snakes, birds, lizards, and scorpions of the area. The many specimens they acquired included 500 marine invertebrates, 147 scorpions, and 61 living fish.

Once the scientists had returned to their museums, the specimens they brought back were studied and the observations made in the field were analyzed. Where warranted, conclusions were reached and distribution began of the new knowledge the scien-

Newly collected invertebrates are examined by two Academy scientists, Chris Parish, foreground, and Dustin Chivers. *Courtesy California Academy of Sciences: photograph, Robert T. Orr*

tists had acquired. Scientific reports were prepared, published, and distributed to museums, libraries, and laboratories throughout the world. Meanwhile the TV film was completed and shown. In addition, an entire issue of *Pacific Discovery*, the Academy's magazine for nonscientists, was devoted to the expedition and its findings. Finally, a number of new specimens were placed on display. The remainder were added to the museum's study collections for future use by its own scientists, scientists from other museums and from universities, and graduate students doing research for advanced degrees.

FOCUS

Hundreds of research trips of all kinds are made every year by museum scientists. In each case, the broad objective is the same: to learn more of man's world. However, as we have seen, the interests of museum scientists vary widely. Here are the major areas with which they are concerned:

BOTANY. Plants, seeds, wood.

ZOOLOGY. Mammals (mammalogy); fishes (ichthyology); animals without backbones, such as jellyfish, worms, clams (invertebrate zoology); birds (ornithology); amphibians and reptiles (herpetology); insects (entomology).

OCEANOGRAPHY. The geography, biology, physics, chemistry, and geology of the oceans.

PALEONTOLOGY. Fossilized life, including plants, fishes, reptiles, mammals.

GEOLOGY. Minerals (mineralogy), rocks, meteorites.

ASTRONOMY. Position, movement, and other characteristics of the heavenly bodies.

ANTHROPOLOGY. Extinct peoples, living primitive peoples.

ECOLOGY. The relationship of living organisms to their environment.

Of course, few museums deal with all these subjects. The smaller ones such as the Dayton Museum of Natural History in Ohio and the Cranbrook Institute of Science in Bloomfield Hills, Michigan, concentrate on the plant and animal life and geology of their regions. The very largest museums, on the other hand, have extremely broad interests and conduct research all over the world. These museums include the Smithsonian's Museum of Natural History in Washington, D.C., the American Museum of Natural History in New York, the Field Museum of Natural History in Chicago, the Milwaukee Public Museum in Wisconsin, and the Los Angeles County Museum of Natural History.

In a recent year a scientist from the Los Angeles County Museum was in Uganda collecting specimens of plant and animal life in a vast forest that was to be destroyed and replaced with tea plantations. At the same time another museum scientist, an ichthyologist from the Field Museum, was collecting fishes from the waters of the Pacific Ocean off Chile and Peru. In the Rocky Mountains a paleontologist from the American Museum of Natural History was excavating the fossils of fish that swam there in an inland sea 200 million years ago. Meanwhile, Smithsonian anthropologists were in Mexico excavating the sites of ancient villages and in a remote section of Brazil studying the life of a vanishing Indian tribe.

A museum scientist usually has two goals on a research trip. One is to learn as much as possible about his subject from what he can observe. The other is to gather specimens to expand his museum's reference collections. In fact, collecting often may be the primary reason for a trip. To study virtually anything in nature, a scientist in a museum must have samples to which he can turn much as he would turn to books in a library. The reference collections are designed to meet this need. The larger and more complete they are, of course, the better they serve. Assembling such collections and preserving and classifying them is one of a museum's major responsibilities; identifying species and types not previously known is another. Taking inventory of nature in this way is known as taxonomy. Once such a collection has been organized— be it minerals or meteorites, plants or snakes, that are involved—it serves as a permanent record of one part of man's natural environment. As such it also serves as a kind of standard to which researchers can turn to identify the specimens they collect. Moreover, it is a continuing source of new knowledge as researchers study and compare specimens.

If one is interested in the birds of a particular country, for example, he might consult the American Museum of Natural History, which has a reference collection of over 800,000 birds from all over the world. If it is minerals one is studying, he might visit the Museum of Natural History in Washington where there are over 1,800 kinds on file; if it is human bones, he might try that museum's Anthropology Department, which has collected enough to fill 10,000 drawers. If the subject is Pacific Coast reptiles and amphibians, at last count there were 100,500 specimens available for inspection at the California Academy of Sciences.

It is likely that most people would be satisfied with seeing just a few birds or minerals or bones or snakes, that thousands really would not be necessary. The scientist, on the other hand, wants to see as many as possible. It is only in this way, with the evidence of nature's variety before him, that he can begin to understand differences and relationships and see a species for what it truly is.

Some fields of study have been completely inventoried and classified. Thus, all of the world's birds are now known. It is estimated, however, that 70 per cent of the plant life of South America has not been described. The same situation exists with salt water fish. As many new varieties are being described today as was the case a hundred years ago. In fact, when I visited the Field Museum in Chicago the curator of fishes, Loren P. Woods, was in the midst of identifying unknown varieties of squirrel fishes in the Pacific and Indian oceans. He had several thousand preserved specimens in his laboratory and was carefully contrasting them with one another. Using calipers, he measured the overall length of each fish, as well as the length of its head, snout, and upper jaw. He also measured the depth of its body, the width between its eyes, and the size of its fin and gill rays. Then he counted the rays, the number of scales, the number of rows in which scales occurred, and the number of gill rakers the fish used to strain its food. A long column of figures on each fish was the result. In the end, with

Dr. Jack Fooden of the Field Museum's Zoology Department checks measurements on the museum's collection of monkey skulls. *Courtesy Field Museum*

enough columns on enough fish, similarities and differences would become clear.

Insects also are largely unknown. It is estimated that for every insect that has been described, ten have not. The week before I talked with Dr. Charles L. Hogue, curator of insects at the Los Angeles County Museum, he had identified a fly which previously was unknown. It is shown in its various parts on page 184. Dr. Hogue found nothing quite like it in all the published descriptions of flies. It differs from others in its shape, in the number of its hairs and bristles, in the relative size of various parts of its eyes, and in other ways as well. He named it *Diotopsis* (for its category) *alpina* (for Lake Alpine in Alpine County, California, where it was collected).

If increasing our understanding of nature is not sufficient reason to maintain collections, there are "practical" reasons as well.

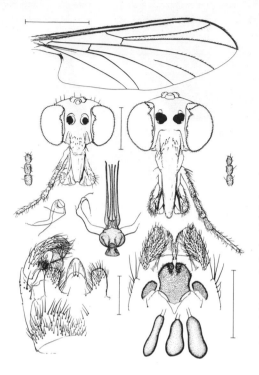

The various parts of
Diotopsis alpina, a
previously unknown fly
identified at the Los
Angeles County Museum
of Natural History.
The drawings are greatly
enlarged; actual size
is indicated by vertical
lines. *Courtesy Los
Angeles County Museum
of Natural History*

Insect collections are a source of help to health and customs officials in their efforts to identify harmful insects. Oil companies sometimes turn to museum paleontologists for help in identifying tiny fossils which drilling rigs may bring to the surface; the right kind indicate that oil is nearby. When a particularly resistant form of malaria turned up in Vietnam, the United States Government sent out a call for samples of Asian mosquitoes so that it could study the problem. The California Academy of Sciences was able to send twenty thousand specimens to Washington which it had collected and preserved twenty years earlier.

Perhaps the most dramatic example of how a collection serves occurred during World War II. An unexploded Japanese incendiary bomb was found on the West Coast with grains of sand clinging to it. The sand was sent to the Museum of Natural History in Washington for possible identification. With the help

of a reference collection, it was determined just where the sand—
and the bomb—came from.[2]

Today natural history museums are also concerned with matters
other than identification and classification. One of their growing
interests is ecology. Another is oceanography. A third is animal
behavior. One of the centers for research in the latter field is the
American Museum of Natural History where scientists have been
studying questions such as these: Why do tropical ants line up in
columns when they go hunting? How well do birds see and tell
time and to what extent can they navigate by the stars? What is the
vocabulary of a frog? What are the biological responses of man to
extreme crowding?

BEGINNINGS

The nation's first museum, formed in 1773 by the Library Society
of Charleston, South Carolina, also was the nation's first natural
history museum. Although at the outset it had no collections, it
did have an acquisitions committee that had lots of optimism. The
committee asked local citizens to provide specimens of ". . . the
various Fossils, Minerals, and Ores, the different Soils, Earths,
Clays, Marles, Stones, Sands, [and] Shells . . ." It also sought
"every species" of animal life, as well as plants of "every kind,
from the Loftiest Tree in the Forest, to the smallest Plant of the
Fields. . . ."[3] Our old friend Charles Willson Peale was also
intrigued by nature. Along with the many portraits in his
museum, there were, you will recall, many natural history exhibits. The ticket of admission gave a sense of what to expect.
"The Birds and the Beasts will teach them!" it proclaimed.
"Admit the bearer to Peale's Museum containing the wonder-ful
works of nature and the curious works of ART." The wonderful
works of nature were represented for most part in Peale's collection of stuffed animals, many of which he prepared and positioned

[2] Karp, *The Smithsonian Institution*, p. 45.
[3] W. M. Smallwood, *Natural History and the American Mind*. New York:
Columbia University Press, 1941, pp. 109–10.

himself in displays depicting their natural habitats. In doing so, he anticipated by almost a hundred years an approach other museums would come to use. He also carried out the first scientific expedition in behalf of an American museum when in 1801 he journeyed to an upstate New York farm where he excavated the remains of several mastodons. He then assembled two skeletons, displayed one at his museum and sent the other on a tour of England with his son Rembrandt. A few years later he depicted this achievement in a painting he called "Exhuming the First American Mastodon," probably the only time a paleontologist has taken such a step. The painting is displayed in the Peale Museum in Baltimore.

In this period, many amateurs also were collecting natural history specimens for their private pleasure, attempting to arrange them in some logical way, then displaying them in "cabinets" in their homes. It was through the efforts of such collectors that the Maryland Academy of Sciences was founded in Baltimore in 1797. Its modern-day descendant is a natural history museum of the same name. Fifteen years later amateur collectors organized the Academy of Natural Sciences of Philadelphia and its museum, both of which are still in operation.

The influence of government began to be felt in the 1830's as a number of states undertook surveys to determine what their natural resources were. In the process, specimens of rocks, minerals, fossils, and plant and animal life were gathered which would serve as the basis of various museums. Using such material, in 1843 New York State formed a "State Cabinet of Natural History" which later grew into the New York State Museum of Natural History in Albany. Right after the Smithsonian Institution was established in 1846, it began assembling what in short order became the nation's major natural history collections. Its specimens were gathered largely by amateurs. Some were members of government expeditions and surveying parties that were exploring unknown sections of the country. The Smithsonian equipped them with guidebooks, scientific instruments so that accurate readings and measurements

After Charles Willson Peale excavated the remains of several mastodons, he depicted his achievement in this painting "Exhuming the First American Mastodon." The large wheel is part of a pumping system used to drain the site. At the base of the wheel a workman holds up a leg bone. At the right, Peale and three of his sons, Rembrandt, Rubens, and Raphael, unroll Peale's full-scale drawings to identify it. At least twenty of the figures in the painting are portraits of Peale's family, relatives, and friends, although most were not present. *Courtesy Peale Museum Baltimore: gift of Mrs. Harry White*

could be made, and also with advice on the fine art of "skinning out" birds so that skins in proper condition could be obtained. A network of other amateurs throughout the country also sent in specimens from the areas where they lived. In addition, there was a corps of young scientists who came to work at the Smithsonian without pay, there being no money available for them at the time, who explored and collected in its behalf as far away as Alaska. The harvest was enormous. Just after the Civil War, in fact, the Smithsonian was able to organize major exhibits on biology, geology and fossils, and Indian life.

Meanwhile, amateur naturalists on the West Coast had formed the California Academy of Sciences in San Francisco in 1853. What is remarkable is that at the time the city itself was only seven years old and not exactly the kind of place one would expect to find an interest in scholarship. In fact, only three years later the academy's founder and first president, Dr. Andrew Randall, was murdered in his bed by a gambler. Although this had little effect on the growth of the organization, in 1907 it suffered a severe setback when the San Francisco earthquake and fire destroyed its building and its collections and, after fifty years of work, it had to start over.

It was in 1862 during the Civil War that the nation acquired its first and most famous medical museum, the museum of the Armed Forces Institute of Pathology in Washington, D.C. The museum was organized to collect and preserve specimens of injuries suffered on battlefields to help physicians in reducing the number of war deaths in the future. No curator ever faced a more unpleasant assignment. To collect the first of his specimens, Major John Hill Brinton visited battlefields, retrieved discarded arms and legs that had been amputated, preserved them in whiskey when nothing else was available, and carted them back to Washington.

The 1860's also saw the establishment of major natural history museums at Harvard and Yale and the founding of New York's American Museum of Natural History. It came into being in 1869, a result of the determination of its first director, Dr. Albert S. Brickmore, and the wealth of such men as J. Pierpont Morgan, the multimillionaire who also helped the Metropolitan Museum of Art; Robert Colgate, the soap manufacturer; A. G. Phelps Dodge, a mining mogul; and Morris K. Jesup, also a financier. For eight years the museum occupied what is today the Armory in

Central Park. Then it moved to its present quarters which have grown and grown. The museum now occupies nineteen buildings joined together, twenty-three acres of floor space, and four city blocks.

Chicago's famed Field Museum was established in 1893 with natural history exhibits that earlier had been brought to the city for a world's fair and a gift of a million dollars from the merchant Marshall Field. Along with its newly acquired collections and wealth, one of the museum's most important assets was Carl Akeley, the great naturalist, animal sculptor, and taxidermist, who earlier had been with the Milwaukee Public Museum. Akeley became famous for his realistic habitat groups of mounted animals. His first life group, a display of muskrats completed in 1892, still may be seen at the Milwaukee Museum. It is shown on page 189. At the Field Museum his best known work is a pair of giant elephants in the museum's Great Hall. In 1909 he moved to the American Museum of Natural History, where today Akeley Hall preserves his later works and his memory.

This diorama of muskrats at the Milwaukee Public Museum was the first such life group done by the famed taxidermist Carl Akeley. It was completed in 1892. *Courtesy Milwaukee Public Museum.*

One of the most important developments in the story of natural history museums occurred in 1921 when the first of the National Park Service's trailside museums was opened in Yosemite National Park in California. To help visitors better understand what they have come to see, the Park Service today maintains approximately a hundred such units. Each is concerned with interpreting a natural area or a section once occupied by early peoples.

The first years of the twentieth century also were the time of the great museum expeditions into little known regions of the world. A number of such undertakings were organized by the American Museum of Natural History. One took museum scientists to the North Pacific where their research confirmed that thousands of years earlier there had been a land bridge over which men migrated from Siberia to North America. On another expedition a team of ornithologists spent the better part of a decade in the South Seas gathering specimens of the birds of that area. A third, the Eastman-Pomeroy-Akeley Expedition to Africa, brought the museum its great collection of African mammals. The most spectacular of these expeditions, however, was Roy Chapman Andrews' eight-year exploration of the Gobi Desert in Outer Mongolia. Forty men were involved—experts in geology, fossils, mammals, reptiles, and fishes—as were eight trucks and a caravan of one hundred camels. Andrews' finds were extraordinary. The most remarkable was a dinosaur breeding ground where excavations turned up more than seventy fossilized dinosaur eggs and a group of thirteen skulls which show in one type of dinosaur its development from an embryo to a full-size adult.

Today's research trips usually are on a much smaller scale. Perhaps the only current exception is a series of long-term studies of the world's oceans. One three-year effort in the Pacific involved twenty nations and forty-four ships. Otherwise, one or two men and a few weeks or months usually are all that a project requires. Occasionally, as was the case in Baja California, a larger group is necessary, but rarely is more time needed.

Although scientists out in the field may sleep in tents, some I've

Roy Chapman Andrews examines fossilized dinosaur eggs discovered in 1925 in the Gobi Desert on an expedition for the American Museum of Natural History. The eggs point toward the center of the nest just as they were left by the mother dinosaur a hundred million years earlier. *Courtesy American Museum of Natural History*

talked with prefer to drive back to an air-conditioned motel room for the night. There also is another difference. More often than not these days, a scientist knows what he is looking for and has a good idea of where to find it. In the great expeditions of the past, less was known, more was sought, and a far wider net was cast.

At any time, however, expeditions are not without danger. James A. Oliver, director of the American Museum of Natural History, recalls that Dr. Andrews saved his party from an ambush of Mongol bandits by driving his touring car into their midst at high speed, and that on another occasion bandits were frightened off when one of the scientists plucked out his artificial eye. On a trip to Africa, Carl Akeley saved himself from an attacking leopard by strangling it. More recently, one of the museum's staff members was shipwrecked on the Great Barrier Reef near Australia and another was cornered for a time by a shark in an underwater canyon where he was examining a coral reef.[4]

GIFTS, GRANTS, AND COLLECTIONS

Research trips are paid for in various ways. Those that don't take a scientist very far from home may be met out of a museum's funds for day-to-day expenses. Other trips may be paid for with income from an endowment fund just for research. In other cases, gifts may cover the costs involved. The Field Museum, for example, recently received a $21,000 gift toward the expenses of a zoological expedition to Afghanistan and another gift of $600 to help pay for botanical research in Central America. Occasionally a museum will acquire a supporter, or patron, who undertakes expeditions on his own, then gives the museum what he acquires. Thus a lawyer in Saint Paul, who also is an amateur anthropologist, has collected specimens for the city's Science Museum on a number of trips he has made down the Amazon. At the Seattle Museum of History and Industry several of the mammals displayed are the gift of a big-game hunter. At times, someone who wants to help in this way will work very closely with the museum and may arrange to have members of the museum staff accompany him as his guests.

At the Los Angeles County Museum of Natural History the magnificent life group of elephants and other animals, which is shown on page 193, is the result of such an effort. In this case two wealthy big-game hunters were involved, both members of the museum's board of governors. One was Maurice A. Machris, a retired oil refiner; the other was the late Tom A. Knudsen, who operated a dairy firm. During a four-month safari to Kenya in East Africa, on which their wives accompanied them, they acquired not only elephants but thousands of additional specimens for the museum's collections, including families of chimpanzees and

---

4 "Behind New York's Windows on Nature," *National Geographic*, February, 1963.

The specimens for this magnificent life group at the Los Angeles County Museum of Natural History were gathered in East Africa by two of the museum's wealthy supporters. *Courtesy of Los Angeles County Museum of Natural History: photograph, Armando Solis*

monkeys, and birds, insects, and plants. The museum's representative was its senior taxidermist, George Adams, who helped select the animals needed for the life group in terms of a model he had created earlier, prepared their skins in the field, and made the complex measurements necessary to mount them properly. When the animal trackers, professional hunters, drivers, cooks, and other camp personnel are taken into account, over sixty people were involved in the expedition.

The major financial support for museum research, however, comes from agencies of the Federal government. The usual procedure is for a museum to apply to a particular agency for a grant of funds to cover the cost of a specific project. Then the application is approved or rejected based on what the project is, the cost, and other factors. The most active of these Federal agencies is the National Research Foundation whose purpose is to encourage basic research. The largest number of its grants naturally go to museums with the largest research staffs. In 1965, for example, the foundation gave the Museum of Natural History in Washington the money needed to undertake fifty-four research studies, including one on "Taxonomy of Bamboos" and another on "Environment of Permo-Triassic Reptiles of the Order Therapsida in South Africa." However, it also granted funds that year to pay for botanical research at the far smaller Cranbrook Institute of Science in Michigan. Other government agencies that support museum research include the Atomic Energy Commission, the National Institutes of Health, the Army Medical Research and Development Command, the Office of Naval Research, and the Naval Training Devices Center. Additional help sometimes is provided by private foundations. Thus the small Belvediere Scientific Fund paid for over half the cost of the expedition to Baja California by the California Academy of Sciences.

Research grants can involve a great deal of money. In a recent year, for example, the American Museum of Natural History obtained $211,700 from the Federal government. In the same period, the Museum of Natural History in Los Angeles received almost $150,000. Many grants enable a museum scientist to do research whose only objectives are to expand man's knowledge and the museum's collections. In other cases research is done on a "contract" basis. A government agency needs information on a given subject and museum scientists try to obtain it. As but one example, curators of insects at the Los Angeles Museum, the Field Museum, and the Museum of Natural History in Washington all have received grants from the Army to study disease-carrying insects in parts of the world of strategic importance. If the Army ever has to send troops into such areas, it then would be prepared to deal with the diseases that might be encountered.

Research is but one of the ways a museum acquires its collections. In a six-month period The Science Museum in Saint Paul was given the following: an albino pocket gopher, a collection of Dakota Indian costumes and utensils, a coquina slab containing invertebrate fossils, a pair of Indian moccasins, a Dakota Indian hat band, two specimens of copper ore, the costume of a Guatemalan woman, a brass container from India, and a musk ox skull. Two of the most magnificent collections at the American Museum of Natural History also were gifts. One is a collection of gems given by J. Pierpont Morgan, some of which were stolen from the museum, then recovered, a few years ago.[5] The other is a collection of 280,000 birds donated by Mrs. Harry Payne Whitney; her husband, in turn, provided the money for a new wing to house them. Perhaps just as pleasing to the museum, although in quite a different way, was a gift in 1965 of three hundred turtles, lizards, and frogs collected and contributed by a school boy in Bangkok.

During recent years a growing number of universities have turned their natural history collections over to neighboring museums with the understanding that their faculty and students could continue to use them as necessary. The largest such shift occurred when the Walker Museum of Paleontology at the University of Chicago gave the Field Museum its fossil invertebrates. So vast was the collection that the National Science Foundation gave the museum $875,000 to build an area in which to house it.

When funds are available, and often they are not, museums also may purchase the collections and specimens they need. Sometimes large sums are involved, but not always. At the Los Angeles County Museum of Natural History, the curator of insects will pay from two cents up to fifty cents for specimens he needs. Museums also borrow from other museums. In addition, where they have something they don't need that another museum does, they arrange trades.

No matter how a museum obtains its possessions, in the end virtually everything it owns was collected at some time by someone and the methods involved often are fascinating. As examples, let's consider how a dinosaur is collected and also insects, fish, and the artifacts of ancient American Indians.

COLLECTING A DINOSAUR

The dinosaur discussed here is of the Triceratops variety, a bulky, barrel-shaped creature that moved about on four massive legs, was

[5] See "How Museums Are Protected," Chapter 1.

twenty-six feet long, almost ten feet high, and weighed over six tons. As all of its kind, it had an enormous head, the largest ever possessed by a living creature. In the case of our Triceratops, it measured 7 feet, 3 inches from the tip of its beak to the bony frill at the back of its neck. Out of its head grew the three horns for which it is named. Two sprang from its brow just over its eyes; the third jutted from its nose. Its skeleton is displayed in The Science Museum in Saint Paul, about 750 miles from northeastern Montana where the dinosaur died between 63 and 70 million years ago. Its death occurred toward the end of the Cretaceous period when dinosaurs were becoming extinct and mammals had begun to appear. Then Montana was a tropical lowland of streams, mudflats, and swamps choked with vegetation.

When a creature died and its remains were not disturbed, it eventually became buried in this ooze. Much later in time the mud and sand in which it lay became shale and sandstone. If glaciers, volcanos, and earthquakes did not disturb the area and if erosion did not expose the burial site, the skeleton of the dead animal would survive as a fossil. This is what happened to Triceratops. By modern times, its burial site had become a hilly, eroded area of buttes and gullies. Now its remains lay near the surface of a butte. Each year, as the ground froze, then thawed and heaved, and as rain fell and ran down the sides of the butte into the gullies below, more and more of the surface was worn away. Finally portions of the fossil itself were exposed and fragments of its bones also were washed into the gullies.

Bruce Erickson, the paleontologist at The Science Museum, began his search for a dinosaur in 1959. He had two objectives: one was to learn more about the environment of the last dinosaurs; the other was to collect a dinosaur the museum could display. With the guidance of geologic maps and the experience of previous exploration, Mr. Erickson examined outcroppings of Cretaceous rock in North and South Dakota, Wyoming, and Montana. Finally, in the Hell Creek area of Montana, some thirty miles north of Jordan, he found enough fossil-bearing rock to convince him that this was a likely place to try. The following year he returned to Hell Creek with a crew of twelve, mostly students from the University of Minnesota and Macalaster College in Saint Paul. Mrs. Erickson also was along. In fact it was she who spotted a few vertebrae in a gully that turned out to be bone fragments of Triceratops.

Searching for remains involves a large element of luck. There are a great many places to look and one must carefully check them all. In this case the area was divided into segments and two crew members working as a team systematically explored each segment. The trained prospector, of course, can readily distinguish fossils from ordinary rocks and recent bones. The fossils have the intricate detail that stone lacks. Moreover, they are heavy with mineral matter that has seeped into them over the years and they are brittle and dark, whereas other bones are hollow, light in weight, and usually have been bleached white. With enormous good luck one may find a fossilized bone that is the only exposed part of a complete skeleton. Usually what one finds, however, are weathered bone fragments lying on the surface to which they have been carried from higher ground by rain. Where such fragments appear promising, the paleontologist will attempt to determine where they came from. If he is fortunate he will find a trail of such fragments which lead up the side of a butte. Most often, however, fragments lead nowhere, and even when there appear to be trails, they may be false.

After the search in Montana had been under way for two weeks, Mrs. Erickson made her find. From it bits and pieces of bone led toward the top of a butte where still other fragments were found, enough, it was felt, to dig into the butte itself. Day after day more material was uncovered—small and large fragments and complete bones. When a fossil was found, probes and brushes were used to gently clear the earth from around it. As the upper portion was exposed, it was coated with dilute shellac to harden its fragile surface. When the top, the ends, and the sides had been coated in this way, tissue paper was shellacked onto the bone as further

Top: One of the two sites in Montana from which paleontologists recovered a skeleton of the horned dinosaur Triceratops which is displayed at The Science Museum in Saint Paul, Minnesota. Bottom: Bones and bone fragments encased in plaster are packed for shipment. *Courtesy The Science Museum*

protection. Then burlap strips soaked in plaster were added until the exposed portion was tightly enclosed. When the plaster dried, the researchers tunneled underneath, turned the section over, and also wrapped that side in plaster strips. The result was a kind of cast, much like one that might be used to support a broken arm or leg. By the end of the summer it was clear that at least a partial skeleton had been found. Digging continued the following summer and also the one after that. When the fossils finally were exhausted at the first site, the researchers turned to the site of still another skeleton which required two more seasons to excavate. In the end, over two hundred dinosaur bones were jacketed in plaster, packed in crates, hauled to Jordan, then shipped by truck back to Saint Paul.

As it turned out, both skeletons were those of young Triceratops dinosaurs. Each would contribute parts to the dinosaur to be displayed. But before a display could be assembled two years of laboratory work were needed. The bones had to be removed from their jackets, then carefully cleaned of foreign matter, then repaired and restored where necessary. At times only fragments of a bone were available to work with. These had to be painstakingly pieced together and glued in a process that often took weeks. Where sections of a bone were missing, plaster was used as a filling, then tinted the color of the bone.[6]

When the bones finally were ready to assemble, another time-consuming process began. It had been decided to support the dinosaur with steel rods that wherever possible would be concealed inside the bones. To do this, a hole had to be drilled by hand through the length of each bone involved. Then steel plates had to be positioned between each vertebra, and these, in turn, had to be welded to steel bars running the length of the body.

In all, over seven years were involved in collecting and preparing the dinosaur. The result is a remarkable exhibit. The skeleton

[6] In some museums, such as the Museum of Natural History in Washington, restored areas are left white to distinguish them from the bone.

Top: The skeleton is painstakingly re-created on a metal frame.
Bottom: The completed skeleton. *Courtesy The Science Museum*

is one of but three of the Triceratops family displayed in the United States. The others are at the American Museum of Natural History and the Smithsonian's Museum of Natural History. However, each of those specimens is composed of the bones of several dinosaurs of more than one species. The dinosaur at Saint Paul is considerably more accurate in that it is a composite of but two skeletons of the same species.

One of the interesting things about the Saint Paul dinosaur is a puncture wound just below its left eye socket. It might have been inflicted by the horn of another Triceratops or even by a six-inch dagger tooth of an enormous, fearsome Tyrannosaur. Because it looks so fierce itself, however, the Triceratops has acquired a nickname in Saint Paul. It is called Fafner after the dragon in Richard Wagner's opera *Siegfried*.

COLLECTING INSECTS

Instead of acquiring one specimen over a period of years, the entomologist may add as many as five hundred to his collection in a single day. He uses a net to capture flying insects and usually picks up the others he needs with his hand. Whenever a capture is made, the insect and others like it are dropped into a killing jar which has cyanide crystals at the bottom that give off a poisonous gas, and the jar is sealed and labeled. Of course one finds insects virtually everywhere—in the air, in the water, in the ground, on plants, and under the bark on trees. The entomologist who is after a particular kind of insect naturally heads for its habitat. Thus Dr. Charles Hogue of the Los Angeles County Museum of Natural History does much of his collecting in and around waterfalls where a fly he specializes in spends its days.

Finding what one is after isn't always easy, though. In the dry Southwest there are many insects which appear only when food is available. What complicates matters is that the food itself may appear only at certain times—thus, some plants may emerge only after a rainful. As another example, one group of moths lays their eggs only on certain plants. These plants bloom in the spring, but only when there has been sufficient moisture the preceding winter. Some years the plants don't grow and the moths don't appear. There also are other challenges. In collecting disease-bearing parasites, for example, Dr. Hogue first had to capture and kill the creature on which the parasite lived, usually a rodent or a bat. Then he placed the dead animal under a microscope and went over it inch by inch, using fine forceps to pick off the parasites he otherwise could not see. As noted earlier, museum-trained volunteers also add specimens they have found to its collections. When I interviewed Dr. Hogue, he had the help of two Peace Corps workers in Kenya and a man in Lake Tahoe, California, all of whom sent in regular shipments.

After an insect is captured, it is dried. Since insects have their skeletons on the outsides of their bodies, once their soft innards have decayed, the hard outer shell lasts indefinitely. Then a label is prepared and a lacquered steel pin is run through both the label and the insect's body. It serves as a handle so that the insect itself need never be touched.

COLLECTING FISHES

The great international studies of the oceans in recent years have involved a massive collecting program in which specimens of all types have been gathered. They are being used in research on the kinds of marine life, their numbers, and their distribution. A good example of the techniques used in such collecting is offered by a voyage the *Anton Bruun,* a National Research Foundation vessel, made in 1965 in the southeastern Pacific.[7]

The objective was to collect specimens of animal and plant life at all levels of the ocean, from the deepest parts to the tidepools. Depending on the fish and the circumstances, the equipment used included diving gear, set lines, traps, and trawling nets measuring some forty feet wide and forty feet long. The nets were

[7] A report by Loren Woods of the Field Museum in the museum's February, 1966, *Bulletin* is the source of this account. Mr. Woods journeys to far places at least once a year in search of specimens.

lowered and raised with enormous electric winches. During the day they would be sent four miles to the ocean's bottom where for periods of thirty minutes at a time they would be dragged behind the ship. Then they would be hauled up, emptied, and sent back down. In the early evening they would be set out again, this time to sample the various levels of the midwaters. When a net was hauled in, its contents were transferred to deep trays where scientists would inspect them and select samples of the most useful specimens. The fish selected were photographed and placed in a preservative. When they hardened, they were wrapped in cheesecloth, packed in plastic bags, and placed in containers for shipment. For each sample a record was made of the location at which it was taken, the depth and temperatures of the water, and the character of the ocean bottom. Just before trawling began in the early evening, a trap, a deep set line with fifty to a hundred baited hooks, and a weighted buoy were sent to the bottom, where they were left overnight. When a twelve-hour fuse burned through the next morning, the weight was released and the buoy, the line, and the trap returned to the surface. There they were located by radar or, if the waves were too high, by birds trying to get at the fish on the hooks. Some of the fish collected were shipped directly to the museums and other institutions involved. The rest went to the Smithsonian's Oceanographic Sorting Center in Washington where the staff sorts and processes specimens and makes them available to scientists who need them for research.

COLLECTING ANCIENT INDIAN ARTIFACTS

In the Tocks Island area of the Delaware River in northern New Jersey, archaeologists from the New Jersey State Museum are engaged in a race against time. In 1972 the section is to be flooded in developing a national recreation area. By then, the museum hopes to have completed research which will provide a picture of how the Indians who occupied this area lived and worked from prehistoric times, beginning perhaps 7000 B.C., until the coming of the white man. In the process, the arrowheads, pottery, hoes, net sinkers, and other implements the Indians used, along with early skeletons, are being retrieved for preservation, study, and display in the anthropology section at the museum. The excavations, financed largely with Federal funds, are headed by a twenty-seven-year-old woman, Patricia Marchiando.

In a recent summer Miss Marchiando and a crew of fourteen high school and college students explored six sites along a four-mile stretch of the river. When the sites were selected they all appeared to be the kinds of places where early Indians might have settled. They had good drainage, good sources of fresh water, and were high enough above the river not to be flooded. In addition, in a number of cases, nearby farmers had turned up significant artifacts in plowing their fields.

One of the first steps after deciding on a site was to divide it into five-foot squares and then select one square at random in which to dig a test pit. Depending on what is found, as many as three or four test pits may be dug on a single site. The excavators dig down six inches at a time. If nothing is found they dig another six inches. If they reach thirty-six inches without finding anything, they start another pit. In other cases, a single pit may be extended if excavation is fruitful. For each level in a pit there is a specimen bag to hold whatever is found. The bag is identified by the site, the pit and level numbers, and the stratum number. Soil occurs in layers of different colors, with each layer an indicator of age. The stratum number tells which layer of soil is involved. Using specimen bags in this way later helps the archaeologist to reach conclusions about the kinds of lives Indians were leading in various periods.

In one test pit at the eighteen-inch level excavators found the charred remains of a fire pit with cracked stone at the bottom. Post holes showing where posts had been placed to support tepees also were found. They were identified as post holes because the soil inside them was darker than that around it and was round like a post. Top soil that was pushed into the ground when the post was

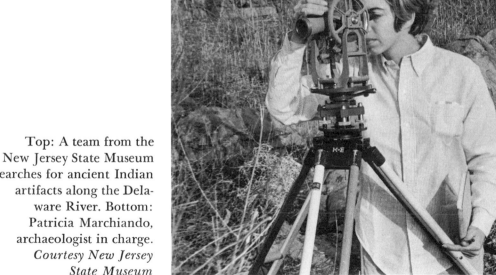

Top: A team from the New Jersey State Museum searches for ancient Indian artifacts along the Delaware River. Bottom: Patricia Marchiando, archaeologist in charge. *Courtesy New Jersey State Museum*

inserted often is what makes the soil darker; decayed wood from the post itself also does. The fire pit and the post holes indicated that a "living floor" or the site of a settlement had been uncovered. The color of the soil and various objects found suggested that at least a thousand years had elapsed since it last was used. At another site in an area high above the river excavators traveled back in time to 3000 B.C. The thick, crudely made soapstone pots discovered at the thirty-six-inch level identified the period.

One of the most productive sites that summer was the so-called "Friedman site" named for the owners of the property. From various pits at the twenty-four-inch level came 200 arrowheads, 33 hide scrapers, 130 fishing net sinkers, hammerstones, pestles, and choppers, and 80 pottery shards or fragments, all dating back two thousand years. From these artifacts it was clear that Indians in that period were hunters, fishermen, and gatherers; this was underscored by the scarcity of pottery. If they had been raising corn and other grain, they would have needed many containers in which to store it.

Where the soil and the objects found do not clearly date a pit level, carbon-14 dating may be used. All material that once was alive, such as bone, vegetable matter, and charcoal from wood, contains radioactive carbon which loses its radioactivity at a known rate. Laboratory analysis can tell just how much radioactivity has been lost, how long it took for this to happen, and, therefore, what the age of the artifact is.

The research at Tocks Island is called salvage archaeology. It is but one of hundreds of similar projects which have been undertaken with the support and leadership of the National Park Service and the Smithsonian Institution. In every case, the objective is to explore important archaeological and historical sites before they are destroyed by dams, highways, pipelines, housing developments, and other construction. The program was organized after World War II, when it became clear that dam construction on the Missouri, Colorado, and Columbia rivers would have such an effect. To date, the Federal government has spent over $2 million in helping to fill in the record of the past in this way. The Smithsonian's Museum of Natural History and state museums in Kansas, Nebraska, South Dakota, and, of course, New Jersey, are but some of the places where what has been salvaged can be seen.

EXHIBITS

In the Museum of Natural History in Washington there is a blue whale ninety-two feet long which gives the distinct impression of having just risen out of icy waters. With its back up, its head down, its tail tensed, at any moment it seems likely to return to the dark depths from where it came. Now almost extinct, the blue whale is the largest creature ever to have lived on Earth. It weighs

A life-size model of the blue whale at the Museum of Natural History in Washington, D.C. *Courtesy The Smithsonian Institution*

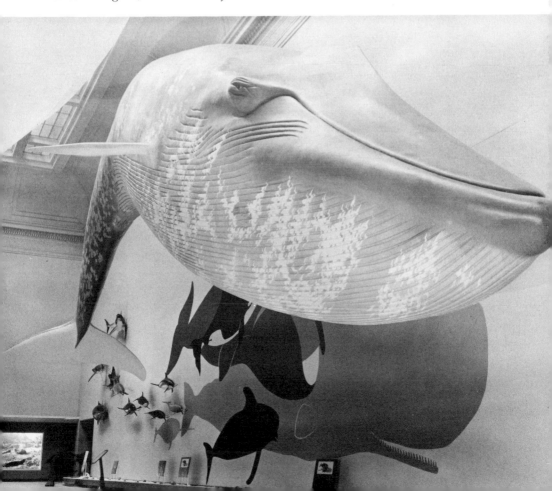

upwards of 150 tons or as much as three of the largest dinosaurs or twenty-five elephants; its flippers are the size of rowboats; its tail is almost as long as a good-sized airplane wing. However, the whale in this museum is plastic, weighs five tons, and is suspended high above the floor on a frame that had to be designed by an aeronautical engineer. A real blue whale captured off Antarctica in 1926 served as the model. Since the skin of the blue whale is laid so tightly over its blubber, the two cannot be separated and the skin cannot be mounted. As a result, if a museum wants to display a whale, a reproduction of one is the only answer. This model took well over two years to create. Months were spent on measurements and statistical studies. Then sketches and designs were made of whales diving, rising, traveling, and blowing. Finally, the design that visitors see today was chosen and construction began. First, two steel brackets were attached to the wall thirty feet above the floor. Then a huge frame was constructed and secured to the brackets. Then the plastic was put on: first, a separating film; next, a gel coat; next, fiberglass cloth. Then, the prefabricated fins were added. Finally, the whale was painted its characteristic blotchy blue color.

That exhibit is a good example of the often costly lengths to which science museums go these days to tell the complex, increasingly exciting story of the world in which we live. At the American Museum of Natural History in New York, one of the pioneers in exhibition techniques, color films, sound, three-dimensional scenes, photographs, and diagrams are used to interpret specimens and their significance. The museum's Hall of the Biology of the Invertebrates is one of the most beautiful and instructive exhibits I have seen anywhere. There are greatly enlarged models in hand-blown glass of the hydroid, the protozoa, and other miniscule creatures that live in the depths of the sea. Elsewhere in the exhibit, models of enlarged fireflies blink overhead, a re-created "automobile" bug of the tropical rain forests turns its headlight-like eyes on and off, and luminous, shrimp-shaped Antarctic krill fade and return to luminosity. At The Science Museum in Saint

This life group at the Milwaukee Public Museum includes sound effects and a mechanical snake that periodically uncoils. *Courtesy Milwaukee Public Museum*

Paul, and at other museums as well, one finds an enormously enlarged model of a DNA molecule, a supremely logical confusion of balls and rods like those that determine what our genetic makeup will be.[8]

At Dinosaur National Monument in Vernal, Utah, the nation's richest horde of fossilized dinosaur bones, visitors watch in a glass-enclosed quarry as technicians armed with pneumatic hammers as well as tiny dental picks outline ancient bones imbedded in the face of a cliff. At the Milwaukee Public Museum one finds a re-created woodland scene in which there are twelve birds whose protective coloration makes them difficult to see. The challenge is to find them. Nearby is a magnificent group of buffalo caught in the act of charging. As one watches he hears a recording of them coming closer and closer, then fading away. In the sagebrush a

[8] DNA stands for deoxyribonucleic acid. The models are so complex that the manufacturer, a Philadelphia firm, sends a man along to put them together. The cost of such a display is about $2,000.

snake periodically uncoils, raises its head, then recoils.[9] At the Cranbrook Institute of Science, the only Atomarium in the Western Hemisphere is used to make atomic and nuclear physics more understandable to the layman.[10] Its equipment includes an operating model of an atom, a Field Emission Electron Microscope, a scintillation viewer, and a cloud chamber. Through its planetarium and observatory, the museum tries to do the same thing with the heavens. The planetarium is one of ninety in the United States which undertake to explain the stars, the planets, the moons, and the latest developments in our knowledge of space.

Science museums everywhere, including the science and industry museums discussed in the next chapter, are confronted with the same problems in their exhibits: keeping up with the rapidly moving flood of new knowledge, translating for the layman the enormously varied and complex ideas it has produced, and taking advantage wherever possible of the many new materials and techniques available in creating exhibits.

In a number of museums new exhibits are being created and old exhibits and entire galleries are being redone in the light of new knowledge. At the American Museum of Natural History, at the Field Museum, and at the Smithsonian's Museum of Natural History, programs of renewal and renovation are under way which eventually will see replacement of all existing halls. Ideally, a gallery should be redone every fifteen years, but most museums cannot afford this. Why they cannot is easier to understand when one realizes that a major gallery may take three to seven years to complete and require anywhere from a quarter to a half million dollars, as well as a sizable staff of experts. The Smithsonian's National Museum maintains the largest museum exhibit staff to meet the needs of both the Museum of Natural

[9] It is hoped that the sudden movement of the snake in an otherwise still area will strengthen the visitor's memory of the exhibit and what it teaches about buffalo and their uses and snakes and the kind of terrain where they may be found.
[10] The only other such installation, the world's first, is in Stockholm at the Tekniska Museet.

The Fels Planetarium at the Franklin Institute in Philadelphia, one of some 90 planetariums in the United States. *Courtesy Franklin Institute: photograph, J. J. Barton*

History, and the Museum of History and Technology. In all, there are 170 specialists on the staff, ranging from designers, artists, illustrators, model makers, and taxidermists to silkscreen workers, photographers, cabinetmakers, and spray painters. Typically, the large natural history museum will have an exhibits staff of from ten to twenty; the smaller museums, on the other hand, may get along with one or two persons, or they may rely completely on the services of outside firms and specialists. In fact, some taxidermists, model makers, and designers on the staffs of the big museums work in their spare time as consultants to the small museums.

A large natural history gallery, just as a major exhibit in a history museum, is based on a script, often a hundred pages or more in length, which has been developed by one or more curators after extensive research. The script sets forth the objectives of the gallery, describes in detail what is to be shown and which specimens and other objects are needed, and provides headings, labels, and other editorial material. Once the script is complete, it goes to a designer who develops a plan, and often a scale model, covering layout, exhibiting techniques, traffic patterns, and the overall appearance of the hall. The design must be approved by the curator and the director and also, at times, by an exhibits committee. Often there are several trips back to the drawing board before agreement is reached. When it is, the specimens and other objects needed are gathered and construction begins.

HABITAT GROUPS

Although museum men disagree as to the educational value of showing mounted animals in a natural setting, there is no disagreement as to the popularity of such exhibits. According to John E. Anglim, chief of the Office of Exhibits at the United States National Museum, they are "the cheesecake" of the museum world. The problem, as he sees it, is that while people enjoy the realism of habitat groups, they don't learn very much from them. There is, of course, a good deal to be learned from such displays about the animals themselves and their relationship to one another and their environment. But Mr. Anglim maintains that most visitors do not approach habitat groups in this way. "Instead," he relates, "they look at the painted backgrounds and say 'What a beautiful painting!' or 'Gee, I can't tell where the grass stops and the painting begins.'"

Whatever people see in such displays, the largest museums and also some of the smaller ones go to a great deal of trouble and expense to be sure that what is shown represents things exactly as they are. On the other hand, where funds are lacking or no purpose would be served by great accuracy, often what one sees are generalized views based perhaps on photographs or color slides.

Those museums that are able to do so may send a scientist into the field along with exhibits specialists and a taxidermist to select the site to be duplicated in a display, to gather the specimens to be shown, and to obtain photographs, sketches, and records to work from. The Museum of Natural History in Washington, for example, recently sent a team of seven men to the highlands of Colombia in South America to obtain what was needed for a new habitat group for the museum's Hall of Botany. At times one man will do the job. This was the case when George E. Peterson of the American Museum of Natural History's exhibits staff did the research and collecting for the museum's Birds of Japan habitat group. He traveled to Japan laden down with all types of equipment: a herbarium press and a formalin tank to preserve plant specimens, tags to catalog and identify them, plaster to make impressions of leaves and flowers that could not be effectively preserved, cameras, various reference books, and a saw and hammer with which to build crates to ship home what he collected. Since it already had been decided to use Mt. Fujiyama as a backdrop for the habitat group, Mr. Peterson first circled the mountain in search of an appropriate site. When he found what he was after, he photographed it in color and in three-dimensional stereo from all angles at ground level. He also made a careful record of the date on which the photographs were made, the time of day, altitude, the weather, and the direction in which the scene lay. Next, he collected, noted, photographed, and preserved or made plaster molds of everything that grew at the site: grasses, mosses, leaves, flowers, shrubs, and portions of trees. He also collected two five-gallon drums of soil. For each specimen he found a matching color in a color atlas to be sure that if fading took place or a specimen had to be reproduced, the right color would be used in the display. Moreover, to make certain that his specimens were properly identified, he hired an interpreter and had them examined by local botanists. Finally, he crated his acquisitions and shipped them to New York.

Often it also is necessary to obtain the animals that are to be shown. In the case of the birds of Japan, however, their skins already were on file in one of the museum's reference collections. This was not the case with the birds of the Great Barrier Reef off Australia. There Mr. Peterson had to trap and kill those he needed and "skin them out"—or remove their skins—in the field. He did this by cutting an opening in the bird's underside, to preserve the feathers, and then separating the skin from the body. However, the skull and the wing and leg bones were left attached to the skin so that later the bird could be properly mounted. Mammals are skinned in a similar way. In collecting bald eagles in Alaska, with government permission, Mr. Peterson found those he needed feeding on dead salmon. He had the eagles shot with a .22-caliber rifle, then had them and the salmon frozen and shipped by air express to New York.

Once the materials for a habitat group have been collected, it next is necessary to reproduce from samples or plaster molds what cannot be preserved. When I visited Mr. Peterson, he was making three hundred blades of manitee grass, a type of sea grass, for an exhibit of ocean life. He first cut the individual blades to size from a sheet of cellulose acetate. Then he sanded them to give the grained effect of the actual grass, attached a wire to the back of each blade as support, and assembled them in the clusters in which they later would be installed in a bed of sand. Where the locale of a display is a woods or a meadow, often it is possible to use real

Top: An artist paints the background setting from a slide for a diorama depicting birds found in the vicinity of Japan's Mt. Fujiyama. Bottom: A completed diorama showing the bald eagle of Alaska and the salmon they feed on. *Courtesy American Museum of Natural History*

grass which has been uprooted. To preserve it and keep it pliable, the grass is soaked in a solution of formalin and glycerin for twenty-four hours. Then the grease is washed off and the grass is spray-painted to maintain the proper color. Next, the blades are set in small cakes of plaster which are dyed the color of the soil in which they are to stand.

The tree leaves in habitat settings usually are reproduced in plastic from a mold of the original. They are made in large quantities with a vacuum-forming device much like a toy one of my children owns. The stems on the leaves are wire; however, the branches from which they "grow" are real. The stems are attached through tiny holes drilled in each branch. Tree trunks are quite a different problem. Sometimes the exterior of an actual tree is used. The tree is cut down and taken to a mill where the outside portions are removed in three or four slabs. Then the slabs are reassembled at the museum, now held together by strap-irons inside the trunk. The tree's branches are fastened to the trunk from the inside. Sometimes, however, the most practical approach is to create a trunk of papier-mâché, using real bark as a model as was done in the exhibit of the streets of Old Detroit at the Detroit Historical Museum.

If water is required in a display, a thick sheet of transparent plastic is used. If the water needs ripples, they are carved into the plastic and the scratches are removed with a buffing machine. If damp ground or mud is necessary, papier-mâché is used; first it is colored, then shellacked. Where small rocks are required, usually real ones are installed. The larger the rock, however, the more likely it is an artificial specimen.

Shadows present another challenge, since those produced by artificial lighting do not accurately represent those at the site. Many museums accept this, but the American Museum of Natural History goes to the trouble of removing the wrong shadows and putting in the right ones, using photographs as a guide. If the surface of the display is solid, paint is applied to make the proper "shadows." If it is sand or soil, the area where the shadows fall is replaced with a material that is light enough so that it blends with the surrounding surface. Once this has been done, "shadows" in the form of a darker surface are added where they should be.

Taxidermy. Few of the "stuffed" animals one sees in museums these days actually are stuffed, but not too many years ago that is precisely what one saw. An animal's skin was tightly filled with cotton batting, cloth, or straw; then the skin was sewn up. The trouble was that stuffed animals never looked quite like the real thing. This approach was replaced by a method Carl Akeley, the taxidermist, developed in the 1920's. After an animal was skinned in the field, he would make a plaster mold of its carcass. From that mold, he would cast a model, or mannequin, of the animal's body to which the skin would be fastened. Although this method still is used in some cases with smaller animals, many taxidermists prefer to create a clay sculpture of the animal's body, based on intricate

Carl W. Cotton, a taxidermist at the Field Museum of Natural History, prepares a baboon for display. *Courtesy Field Museum*

measurements they have made, then cast a mannequin from the sculpture. Some taxidermists also will create a mannequin without casting, using the animal's bones or imitation bones, wire mesh, and papier-mâché.

In recent years a few museums have experimented with a method known as freeze-drying which eliminates skinning and mounting. The dead animal first is arranged in the position in which it is to be displayed. Then it is frozen solid and placed in a vacuum tank where, over a period of weeks, all the frozen moisture in its body is slowly removed. Instead of melting, however, the ice crystals convert directly to vapor. When the specimen is removed from the tank, every drop of moisture in its body has been extracted. As a result, it is said, the animal can be displayed indefinitely at room temperature without danger of spoilage. Thus far the method has been used with animals up to the size of a fox.

All the birds one sees in habitat groups, however, have been "skinned out." In mounting a bird skin, any one of several approaches is used. The taxidermist may make an artificial body of balsa wood, Styrofoam, or excelsior. Or he may use the Akeley method and make a cast of the bird's skinned body. Once the skin is in place, it is secured with dental floss; then wires are inserted into the legs, wings, and neck to hold them in place.[11] Sometimes the fish one sees on display are rubber latex casts made from real fish. However, with larger specimens such as sharks, the original jawbone and teeth are likely to be included.

EDUCATION

Much as the art and the history museums, those concerned with natural history offer an impressive list of educational services. They provide tours for school children, send museum materials to the schools, give teachers special training, and sponsor classes, workshops, and field trips. Where they differ is in the strenuous

[11] Taxidermists also may prepare thousands of animal skins which are not mounted, but are preserved in reference collections for research.

A member of the Student
Section at the California
Academy of Sciences on a
field trip. *Courtesy
California Academy of
Sciences*

efforts they make to encourage bright young people to enter their
field. The Los Angeles County Museum of Natural History, for
example, schedules a series of five-month laboratory courses each
year for the very best high school science students in the area. At
the California Academy of Sciences in San Francisco there is a
Student Section which offers high school boys and girls opportunities to do research and publish papers through the museum. The
summer I visited the Field Museum in Chicago, high-ability high
school students were involved in two programs the National
Science Foundation was supporting. One was a six-week training
program in anthropology involving lectures, laboratory work,
research, field trips, and archaeology. The other involved ten
weeks of training in archaeology at Vernon, Arizona. In New York
that summer, eighty young people spent the month of July in a
free course on astronomy and space science at the Hayden Planetarium. As we shall see, the science and industry museums offer
similar programs concentrating largely on the physical sciences.
However, a number of natural history museums go one step

A teacher at The Science Museum in Saint Paul uses microscopes and closed-circuit television for a lesson. *Courtesy The Science Museum*

further in giving able young people a chance to work in their scientific departments as volunteer helpers on an informal basis. The museums in Los Angeles, Saint Paul, and Milwaukee were three where I found this arrangement.

There also is one museum, the Dayton Museum of Natural History in Ohio, that gives high school and college students full responsibilities in some activities and even pays them salaries. Young people man the sales desk, care for the museum's many live animals, teach museum classes to younger children, lecture to civic groups, collect and classify specimens, and do research. One recent project related to the molting patterns of shrews, another to the mating habits of the corn snake.

Before he reaches fourteen, a youngster can work in the museum as a volunteer. Afterwards he may join the junior staff at a salary starting at fifty cents an hour. The summer I visited there were eight members of the junior staff and a half-dozen volunteers. There also is a junior curator program of long standing in which a boy or a girl may work with one of the museum's curators for as long as a year, learning about his department, helping him, and, with his guidance, developing a research project.

Some years ago the young people in these programs made a contribution that the museum's officials are not likely to forget. At that time, the Dayton museum occupied part of an old warehouse the city had decided to tear down and replace with a parking lot. With little money available to move elsewhere, it appeared that the museum would have to close. Its young workers responded by organizing other youngsters in town into fund-raising brigades. In all, they brought in $25,000—not enough for a new museum, but more than enough to encourage the adults in Dayton to finish the job.

5 | Museums of Science and Industry

UNLIKE THE NATURAL HISTORY MUSEUMS, THE BUSTLING SCIENCE and industry museums with their many do-it-yourself exhibits have neither collections nor curators, nor do they undertake research, nor do they publish learned papers. Their reasons for being are to explain science and scientific advances to the layman, to improve science education, and to interest young people in careers in science and engineering. "If we can attract youngsters who have the ability, but otherwise might not use it," Robert Neathery, director of Philadelphia's Franklin Institute explained, "then we make a contribution to the nation's welfare and security."

The Foucault Pendulum at the Franklin Institute, Philadelphia. *Courtesy Franklin Institute: photograph, Herbert K. Barnett*

BEGINNINGS

The first of the science and industry museums in the United States began operations during the economic depression of the 1930's. The Chicago Museum of Science and Industry, today the biggest of all such institutions, opened its doors in 1933. A few months later the Franklin Institute, a scientific academy dating back to 1824, established its museum as a memorial to Benjamin Franklin. In both, the approach was the same. Instead of cases of specimens to study, there were exhibits visitors could operate. In the process, it was hoped they also would learn something about scientific principles. Through still other exhibits the two museums tried to show how science is used by industry in developing products and services.

The Chicago museum was the result of a millionaire's enthusiasm. He was Julius Rosenwald of Chicago, chairman of Sears, Roebuck and Company. On a trip to Germany in the 1920's Mr. Rosenwald and his eight-year-old son William visited Munich's famed Deutsches Museum which specialized in do-it-yourself exhibits on science and technology. So fascinated were father and son with what they saw, on their return home Mr. Rosenwald urged that such a museum be established in Chicago. As evidence of his interest, he offered to contribute a block of Sears, Roebuck stock worth $8 million. To this, the Chicago Park District agreed to add another $5 million. As a result, when the city's world's fair, the Century of Progress, opened in 1933, the museum opened as one of its pavilions.[1] The Franklin Institute's museum also was a product of great wealth. In just twelve days over $5 million was raised to pay for the museum and its planetarium, with the major contributors including Cyrus H. K. Curtis, publisher of the *Saturday Evening Post,* and Samuel S. Fels, the soap manufacturer, for whom the planetarium was named.

---

[1] Today William Rosenwald and his brother Lessing are honorary trustees of the museum. Lessing Rosenwald also assembled a remarkable collection of prints which he gave to the National Gallery of Art in Washington.

When the Century of Progress came to an end, so did the progress of Chicago's newest museum. Attendance and interest in the project both dropped sharply. To revive the museum it was decided to bring in as director Major Lenox Riley Lohr who had been the chief promoter and manager of the world's fair and had gone on to become president of the National Broadcasting Company. When Lohr agreed to take the job, the museum's trustees were delighted, but Chicago's scientists were not. What would happen, they wondered, to a science museum under the leadership of a promoter and showman? "A tragedy has occurred in the cultural life of our city," the Nobel Prize-winning scientist, Arthur Holley Compton, told newspapermen. Whatever the scientists thought, the public could not have been more pleased. Ten years after Major Lohr took over, attendance had increased to over a million a year. In another ten years it was over two million. Today it is over three million and still climbing. In 1966, in fact, the museum managed to outdraw Chicago's big league baseball, football, basketball, and hockey teams—together. So popular has the museum become with children, a truant officer has been permanently stationed there to spot hookey players who should be in school. However, visitors come from all over. In a typical week during the tourist season forty-nine states and fifty-seven countries were represented. Foreign visitors have included government officials from Spain, Egypt, and Israel who came to find out how they could establish such institutions.

What was it that Major Lohr did to create such a stir? He conjured up what looks like and often sounds like a state fair, cramming his fourteen acres of floorspace with the brightest, most intriguing exhibits he could find. For everyone "from two to toothless," as the major once put it, there are buttons to push, cranks to turn, chains to yank, and levers to pull. When one gets tired of pushing and pulling, he can watch baby chicks hatch, walk through a throbbing sixteen-foot heart, descend into a "coal mine," clamber through a Nazi submarine, inspect the nation's first streamlined train, observe a "steel mill" in operation, or help

A poultry incubator and a device which pops the kernels on an ear of corn with radio waves at Chicago's Museum of Science and Industry.
Courtesy Museum of Science and Industry

invent the wheel. Or he can watch his voice perform on a screen, or he can attend a movie or a science demonstration, or he can sit down and have something to eat. The average visitor remains for three hours and fifteen minutes, about half again as long as he is likely to stay in a conventional museum. However, how much he learns about communication, photography, optics, agriculture, health, medicine, magnetism, electricity, machine tools, or a score of other subjects on which there are displays, is something the museum staff doesn't know. What they are sure of is that people have fun and return again and again.

EXHIBITS

The range of exhibits in all such museums is not only remarkable; it is slightly confusing. The museum in Chicago covers physics, chemistry, mathematics, and the medical sciences, as well as what industry does and how it does it. Boston's Museum of Science goes one step further and also deals with the natural sciences. At the Pacific Science Center in Seattle and the Franklin Institute in Philadelphia the emphasis is on physics and mathematics, but the institute also manages to offer rides in a giant locomotive that travels a six-foot track and in a Link trainer of the type in which pilots train to fly by instruments. The colorful Oregon Museum of Science and Industry in Portland, or OMSI as it is known locally, offers a sampling of all the sciences. So does the California Museum of Science and Industry in Los Angeles.

Frequently the seeming confusion of exhibits is deliberate. By exposing visitors to an organized hodgepodge it is hoped they will have a variety of stimulating experiences which will encourage them to go off and find out more on their own. Often one is stimulated. Sometimes, however, he wishes for the peace and quiet of an art gallery.

At the Chicago Museum of Science and Industry about half the exhibits are prepared by the museum itself or by government agencies such as the Atomic Energy Commission and the National Aeronautics and Space Administration. The rest come from big

A display on mathematical probability in an IBM exhibit at the California Museum of Science and Industry. *Courtesy California Museum of Science and Industry*

American companies like General Motors (the history of wheeled transportation), the Bell System (the story of the telephone plus a chance to talk by "picturephone" to Disneyland), International Harvester (a life-size replica of part of a farm), Eastman Kodak (the uses of photography), the Upjohn Company (a red blood cell magnified a million times), Sears, Roebuck (the story of merchandising), and Union Carbide (animated displays of the chemical elements). One of the most effective and attractive exhibits is IBM's story of numbers which also can be found at the science and industry museums in Seattle and Los Angeles. Created by the designers Charles and Ray Eames, it deals with such matters as probability (which is illustrated by a cagelike machine full of tiny balls), minimal surfaces (which are explained with the aid of a soap bubble machine), and square roots and cube roots (which are defined with the help of a cube made up of light bulbs).

Approximately forty of the largest companies have exhibits in Chicago. The museum's officials say these firms have spent anywhere from $150,000 to $750,000 each, or about $25 million in all. Using exhibits contributed by business organizations is a standard practice at all museums of science and industry. Industry's help is sought largely because working exhibits are very costly and the museums don't have the money to pay for them.

Why are companies interested in spending their money in this way? Many feel a sincere obligation to support an educational program that relates to industry. It is also true, of course, that a firm does benefit from the exposure its name receives when hun-

An exhibit on space flight. *Courtesy Oregon Museum of Science and Industry*

dreds of thousands of people visit its exhibit in a single year. "It is the very best advertising a company can do," D. M. McMaster, director of the Chicago Museum of Science and Industry, told me.

Yet a museum that relies on such help does leave itself open to the pressures of commercialism. In fact, museums of science and industry at times have been criticized for permitting exhibits which contain more information on the sponsor and its activities than is justified. This is not to say that museums don't establish rigid standards to avoid such situations. Usually they retain the right to approve everything in an exhibit, including its design, how the subject is presented, and all the labels and signs. They also insist that no products be mentioned; that no sales claims be made; and that where a sponsor's name is shown, its size meet certain requirements. By and large, they are successful in enforcing such standards. Yet there have been occasions when museums in need of exhibits have relaxed their standards, either by giving a company more recognition than is appropriate or even by using an exhibit that has no place in a museum. When this happens, it shows. I can recall one such exhibit sponsored by a woolen-shirt manufacturer explaining how its products were made. I can recall another sponsored by a gas company demonstrating the benefits of natural gas. Some exhibits on the telephone also fall in this category. All would have been at home in trade fairs where companies try to sell their products and services, but they are out of place in museums.

A museum ordinarily acquires a company exhibit in one of two ways. A firm already may have a display it used elsewhere or a piece of equipment that it is willing to donate. It was in this way that the Franklin Institute acquired several excellent exhibits. Its wonderful operating locomotive was a gift of the Baldwin Hamilton Lima Corporation; its Link trainer was contributed by the General Precision Corporation; its atomic energy exhibit came from the Union Carbide Company which originally displayed it at its New York headquarters. OMSI acquired a DC-3 in this way from Western Airlines, which also installed special seats so that the plane could be used as a classroom.

Often, however, a museum sees a need for an exhibit on a particular subject and seeks out a company to pay the cost of developing it. It often may have to ask many companies before one agrees.

When a company and a museum decide to cooperate in developing an exhibit, a common procedure is to set up a planning committee to handle the details. When General Electric agreed to sponsor an exhibit at the Franklin Institute, the committee consisted of a company representative, a museum representative, and a number of outside electrical engineers who jointly decided on what was needed. Once agreement was reached, the plan was turned over to an exhibits designer who worked closely with the committee. In other cases, a museum may have standing committees of outside experts who develop or closely review plans for exhibits.

A number of museums also create smaller exhibits on their own. As noted earlier, the Chicago Museum of Science and Industry does this. So does Boston's Museum of Science. In fact, in Boston the objective is to build an endowment fund which will produce enough income to give the museum freedom to develop the kinds of exhibits it wants without having to rely heavily on industry. Just a few years ago, using its own funds and working with the guidance of an outside committee of experts, it produced one of the finest science exhibits to be found which deals with how a child is conceived, how it grows after conception, and how it is born.

Describing the complex and the unfamiliar in simple terms is a challenge all science and industry museums face. Ideally such explanations should be understood by anyone of reasonable intelligence, even if he has had no training in science or mathematics. To assure this, a great deal of time may be spent in preparing just a brief label. Even then, a museum doesn't always succeed. At the Franklin Institute, one of the most difficult tasks has been describ-

ing how the Foucault Pendulum actually works. Over a period of
time, the pendulum knocks down a series of carefully spaced pins
in demonstrating that the earth rotates on its axis. Explaining the
operation of a gyroscope is also very difficult. It is easy enough to
understand the principle involved if one also understands calculus, but the trouble is most people do not understand calculus.

The Pacific Science Center in Seattle faces a similar problem
with many of its displays. These exhibits originally served in the
science pavilion of the United States Government at the 1962
Seattle Fair. Although greatly admired in the museum field, the
exhibits are a good example of how green the grass may look from
a distance. The Center's officials have found they are too complicated for the average visitor to readily understand. On the other
hand, one of the most popular displays in the building during the
fair was a science center just for children. Today the equipment

Part of a major exhibit on how life begins. *Courtesy Museum of Science, Boston*

originally intended for them also is enjoyed by adult visitors. As money is available, the museum is slowly simplifying its other exhibits.

Another challenge the science and industry museums face is keeping their do-it-yourself exhibits in operation. Such exhibits break down with distressing regularity under the assault of large numbers of very strong children who push buttons and pull levers with enthusiasm that is hard to believe. As a result, museums take great pains to be sure their operating exhibits are sturdy. They try to be certain, for example, that handles on cranks are not so long they will break off easily and that button mechanisms are strong enough to take heavy punishment.

Film and slide projectors, tape recorders, and other electronic equipment that work on continuous automatic cycles are a source of still other problems. At the Pacific Science Center six men are kept busy full-time making repairs on such equipment. At the Museum of Science and Industry in Chicago four men do nothing but repair projectors.

EDUCATION

Exhibits are but one of the many ways in which museums of science and industry teach. As might be expected, school classes come through in a steady stream. But beyond that the program is extremely varied. OMSI, in Portland, is a good example. For children from six to eight it has offered a Secret Agent Class in which the emphasis was on looking and thinking. Youngsters looked for fingerprints, used a microscope, dealt with disappearing inks, and, from the contents of a woman's purse, tried to deduce who the owner was. For older children, there are courses ranging from stonecutting to astronomy and radio. Once a month, elementary school children participate in a Science Bowl competition. From time to time there are seminars at which the most promising high school science students meet visiting scientists. Soon the museum is to have a laboratory where such young people can work on advanced research projects.

The bernoulli effect is demonstrated for visiting school children at Boston's Museum of Science. *Courtesy Museum of Science, Boston*

The museum also conducts fossil hunts, marine biology collecting trips, spelunking expeditions, and wilderness hikes. During summer months, it runs a series of camps. One such camp is an operating marine biology station. Another is concerned with fossils. A third, at the base of Mount Hood, deals with ecology and studies of volcanic activity. In addition, the museum participates in science fairs, conducts a science talent search in Oregon, and offers science training workshops for teachers. At the California Museum of Science and Industry in Los Angeles there are summer workshops for young people in the Physics of Light and Sound, Radiation Biology, and Energy and the Electron. In addition, six high school students are selected to work throughout the summer on research projects at major laboratories in the area. At the Franklin Institute in Philadelphia one of the major programs takes museum exhibits and demonstrators to schools throughout Pennsylvania. Another is a Science Career Day.

STAFF

Although such museums do not have curators, obviously they do have science educators on their staffs. Most have backgrounds in teaching in high school or in college. In some instances they are key figures in their museums. People who can sell and promote are also extremely important in the science and industry museums since the support of the community and of industry are so essential. Starting with little more than the enthusiasm of a few people in the 1950's, the Oregon Museum of Science and Industry has flourished because of dynamic salesmanship and dedicated amateurs. In fact, all the bricks for its building were laid with donated labor in one remarkable day in 1957 when four hundred bricklayers and hod carriers put 102,000 bricks in place. OMSI's director is a former newspaperman and small-town mayor with a flair for promotion and getting things done. The assistant director, a radio announcer for eighteen years, handles fund-raising and public relations. The education director is a former high school teacher. The exhibits director was a jack-of-all-trades. The museum naturalist was hired as a staff photographer. At the other end of the scale is the Chicago Museum of Science and Industry, a high-powered operation with a staff of 425 that is run with military efficiency. The staff includes exhibits experts, public relations men, a large business staff, and an even larger staff concerned with handling visitors, arranging school tours, and presenting science demonstrations. The director's background is in economics and in printing. He came to the museum the summer it opened to demonstrate printing equipment and has been there ever since.

A Franklin Institute educator heads for schools in the outlying areas with exhibits and demonstrations. *Courtesy Franklin Institute*

Museum Careers:
OPPORTUNITIES, TRAINING, SALARIES

"WHY DO YOU WORK IN A MUSEUM?" I ASKED THIS QUESTION OF people in scores of museums of all types and sizes. Yet the answers they gave did not vary a great deal. People work in museums because art, history, or science fascinates them. They also like seeking out and working with rare and important objects. They enjoy the scholarship, the travel, and the demands on their ingenuity. They like the variety in their jobs, the informality, the kinds of people attracted to museum work, and also the chance to do a public service.

Of course not all museums are equally desirable as places to work. Some are dull and unimaginative. Others are rather rigid and conservative. I have encountered one that was a captive of the social leaders in its city, and another, a publicly owned museum, where the city fathers tried to censor the exhibits.

But from what I have seen, most museums are exceedingly pleasant places where life is stimulating and varied. This appears to be the case whether one is a director, a curator, or a museum specialist such as an editor, a teacher, an exhibits designer, a conservator, a public relations expert, or a librarian.

The primary drawback of a museum career is that, with a few exceptions, museums are financially poor organizations. With increasing government aid, this is slowly changing, but for the forseeable future, it does mean that funds may be quite limited and may depend in large part on the uncertainties of gifts and grants. It also means that salaries may not be as high nor the fringe benefits as generous as they are in other fields. In years past the museum profession had a reputation for being a "rich man's field" in which only a person who already had enough to cover his needs could afford to work. This situation has changed. But despite often valiant efforts by museums, the salaries they pay still lag. While an enthusiastic beginner may take a museum job at any salary just to get started, the progress he makes can be discouraging. Over the

MUSEUM JOBS

DIRECTOR. All museums. Larger museums also may have associate directors, assistant directors, and/or executive secretaries.

CURATOR. All museums except those without collections, such as science and industry museums, health museums, and many junior museums. In smaller museums a director also may serve as curator.

EDUCATOR. Most large and medium-size museums. Exceptions include many historic houses and specialized museums. In such cases, a curator or the director may handle school groups and any other education programs.

REGISTRAR. Most art museums, some history museums. In other cases, including science museums, a curator may serve as his own registrar.

LIBRARIAN. Most large and many medium-size museums. Some science and industry museums are an exception.

CONSERVATOR. The largest art museums. In other cases, consultants handle.

RESTORER OF PAINTINGS, FURNITURE, ETC. Large art museums, a number of large history museums. In many history museums the curator will restore furniture and other objects. In some cases, consultants handle.

EXHIBIT SPECIALIST. All large, some medium-size science and history museums; also some large art museums. In other cases, the director, curators, and consultants handle.

---

years he can anticipate earning a reasonable living, but it is clear that with the same training and experience he would receive a higher income in business, in industry, and often in universities. Whether these jobs would be as satisfying is, of course, another question.

PHOTOGRAPHER. Some large art museums for reproduction of art works, record-keeping, publicity; a few science museums for diorama preparation, publicity.

EDITOR. Some large museums, for magazines, journals, books.

PUBLIC RELATIONS, PUBLICITY SPECIALIST. Most large, some medium-size museums. In other museums, the director, curator, librarian, registrar, membership secretary, or fund raiser will handle.

FUND RAISER. A growing number of large and medium-size museums. At times, duties combined with those of membership secretary and public relations director.

MEMBERSHIP SECRETARY. Larger museums. At times, duties combined with those of public relations and fund-raising.

TV SPECIALIST. Some of largest museums.

PRINTER. Largest museums.

INFORMATION DESK SPECIALIST. Largest museums.

BUSINESS MANAGER, ACCOUNTANT, PURCHASING AGENT. Large museums have a business staff; others may have one person handling all such duties.

MUSEUM SHOP MANAGER, CLERK. Many museums of all sizes.

ENGINEER. Largest art museums. Primary concern is control of humidity and other climatic conditions inside buildings.

MAINTENANCE SPECIALIST. All museums. Larger museums also maintain shops where repairs are carried out.

GUARD. Almost all museums.

Salaries are described in more detail later in this chapter, but generally they are highest in the science museums and lowest in the history museums, highest in the large museums and lowest in the small museums, highest in the Northeast and lowest in the South and the Southwest. For beginners, salaries range from about

$4,000 to $7,000 a year. In the top professional categories the range is from about $10,000 to $16,000. In a few of the larger institutions, directors may have salaries of $20,000 or more. In the very largest and finest museums, directors may command salaries of from $30,000 to $50,000.

With so many new museums opening and so many others expanding, it is not difficult for an inexperienced person with the appropriate training to get a museum job—if he is willing to work where the job is. In fact, many jobs go begging. The largest number of openings for beginners is in the history field, but there also are a significant number each year in art and science museums, although the competition for them may be greater and they may be harder to land.

Generally there are two possible routes to follow in entering the museum field. One is via a job in the small or medium-size museum where a beginner will learn the museum trade from the ground up, doing virtually everything that needs to be done from writing publicity releases and painting signs to helping the curator or director (who may be one and the same) prepare and mount exhibits. Indeed, some persons decide they like the intimacy, variety, and challenge of a small museum and ultimately become directors of such institutions. The day I visited the executive office of the American Association of Museums in Washington, D.C., the placement service there had on file 130 job openings for museum directors, most of them in small museums. Once they have completed their apprenticeship, many beginners move on to larger museums where their experience now makes it easier to get a job and where there is more of a chance to specialize. Following another route, others try to land jobs in the large museums when they leave school, seeking positions as assistants in departments that interest them, or, if need be, filling any opening available just to establish a foothold.

Being a woman does not make a great deal of difference in the opportunities available. Admittedly, few women are directors of large museums. Dixy Ray Lee of the Pacific Science Center in

Seattle, Katherine Coffey of the Newark Museum in New Jersey, and Susan Thurman of the Boston Institute of Contemporary Art are three who are. But many women are directors of small museums and many others serve as curators and in all other museum jobs. Some of the best opportunities for women lie in education, which is one of the best-financed and most rapidly expanding aspects of museum work.

One obstacle that women may face in obtaining a museum job is a feeling among those who do the hiring that they will decide to marry and will leave. Another is that they may not be physically strong enough for certain assignments. Some curatorial jobs require frequent handling of heavy, bulky objects, and for these positions museums sometimes prefer to have men. Museum archaeology is another area where, because of the nature of the work, one finds relatively few women. Instead, women with such an interest may turn to ethnology, the study of primitive groups in existence today, where the emphasis is on interviews rather than on excavation. Yet, as we have seen, the New Jersey State Museum has on its archaeological staff a woman of twenty-seven. She supervises a predominantly male crew of assistants, sleeps in a tent, and even takes her turn trundling a wheelbarrow.

Educational requirements for museum jobs vary with the museum and the field, but in every case requirements have been increasing. In the past it was possible to get curatorial jobs in some museums without a college degree. But this is no longer the case. The minimum requirement for such positions is a bachelor's degree, but a master's degree is preferred. In the largest natural history and history museums, in fact, a Ph.D. degree frequently is required for a curator's position. For other museum jobs at the professional level a college degree also is essential. Of course the more education one has, the better his chance of obtaining a good job and, even more important, of advancing in it. In recent years increasing stress also has been placed on specialized training for museum work. There are a number of courses in museum techniques offered at the undergraduate, graduate, and post-doctoral levels which are regarded as very useful in establishing the basis for a successful career. These are listed later in this chapter. For those who hope to become museum directors, some training in business administration also should be considered.

One of the best introductions to the museum field can be obtained by working as a museum volunteer. Many museums permit college students to work as assistants in various departments or even as lecturers or tour guides. A growing number also have places for able high school students and, in some instances, for junior high school students. Among them are the Minneapolis Institute of Art, the Brooklyn Museum in New York, the Museum of History and Industry in Seattle, the California Academy of Sciences in San Francisco, The Science Museum in Saint Paul, the Milwaukee Public Museum, the Dayton Museum of Natural History in Ohio, and the Museum of Science in Boston. The best way to learn about such opportunities or to find out more about museum careers is to visit the museums in your area and talk with the directors or curators. For a broad picture of the museum field, review back copies of *Museum News,* the excellent monthly magazine issued by the American Association of Museums. It is available in all museum libraries.

The remainder of this chapter deals with the qualifications needed for museum jobs, opportunities for training, and the salaries likely to be offered.[1]

ART MUSEUMS

Curator Training in the fine arts, particularly in art history, is essential. So is a broad cultural background including history,

[1] The salary information is based on interviews with museum directors and other museum personnel. The training opportunities are drawn from *Museum Training Courses in the United States and Canada,* a publication which describes them in detail not practical here. It may be purchased for 25 cents from the American Association of Museums, 2306 Massachusetts Avenue, N.W., Washington, D.C. 20008. Specialties such as public relations, fund-raising, librarianship, and accountancy are not covered in this chapter since they relate to many fields and there is extensive material already available.

literature, and music. In addition, a working knowledge of at least one foreign language, particularly German, French, or Italian, is extremely useful. Since a practiced eye is important in evaluating and purchasing art works, extensive travel and study in museum galleries also is recommended. One art museum director also suggests studio experience in an art school, whether or not an individual has talent. Ordinarily someone interested in curatorial work will take a bachelor's degree in art history, then a master's degree in museum techniques, which usually includes work experience at a cooperating museum.

UNDERGRADUATE AND GRADUATE PROGRAMS

Huntington College Art Department, Montgomery, Ala.

University of Arizona Art Gallery, Tucson

University of California Department of Art, Davis

National Gallery of Canada, Ottawa, in cooperation with Montreal Museum of Fine Arts, the Art Gallery of Toronto, and the University of Toronto's Royal Ontario Museum

Connecticut College and Lyman Allyn Museum, New London

Rollins College Art Department, Winter Park, Florida

College of Notre Dame of Maryland Art Department, Baltimore

Heritage Foundation Summer Fellowships (in early American history and fine arts), Deerfield, Massachusetts

Princeton University Department of Art and Archaeology, Princeton, New Jersey

University of New Mexico Art Gallery, Albuquerque

State University of South Dakota, Vermillion

Richmond Professional Institute, with Valentine Museum and Virginia Museum of Fine Arts, Richmond, Virginia

GRADUATE PROGRAMS

University of Michigan Museum of Art, Ann Arbor, with the Toledo Museum of Art, Toledo, Ohio

University of Delaware, with Winterthur Museum (early American arts and culture)

GRADUATE PROGRAMS (cont.)

University of Minnesota Department of Art, with the University Gallery, the Minneapolis Art Institute, and the Walker Art Center, Minneapolis

University of Missouri Department of Art History and Archaeology, with William Rockhill Nelson Gallery of Art

New York University Institute of Fine Arts, with Metropolitan Museum of Art, New York

Yale University Art Gallery, New Haven, Connecticut

Ford Foundation Museum Curatorial Training Program (predoctoral internships), New York, New York

Fogg Art Museum, Harvard University, Cambridge, Massachusetts

Denver Art Museum, with University of Denver, Denver, Colorado

George Washington University Department of Art, Washington, D.C.

Newark Museum, Newark, New Jersey

American Academy in Rome, 101 Park Avenue, New York, New York

Archaeological Institute of America, New York, New York

Salaries

Beginner, $4,000–6,000; experienced curator, $6,000–12,000; top curatorial positions, $12,000–16,000.

Archaeologist See History Museum Curator.

Educator A bachelor's or master's degree in art history usually is needed, although a few museums will accept a background in cultural or social history plus a strong acquired interest in art. Ordinarily beginners also undergo on-the-job training.

Salaries

Beginner, $4,000–5,000; experienced educator, $5,000–8,000; top education positions, $8,000–12,000.

Restorer, Conservator The restorer of paintings needs an art school background. The conservator of art objects combines an interest in art with an interest in chemistry. He needs an undergraduate education in both fields followed by graduate-level museum training courses. The best is the four-year postgraduate program offered at the Conservation Center of New York University's Institute of Fine Arts. See the listing of Training Opportunities under Art Museums: Curators.

Salaries

Beginner, $6,000–7,000; experienced restorer, conservator, $7,000–12,000; top positions, $12,000–15,000.

Registrar   Undergraduate training in the fine arts and art history is desirable, as is a reading knowledge of French, Italian, or German and a background in business procedures and methods of record-keeping. At present, technical training is acquired on the job. For a sense of the techniques involved, see *Museum Registration Methods* by Dorothy H. Dudley and Irma Bezold, published by American Association of Museums.

Salaries

Beginner, $5,000–6,000; experienced registrar, $6,000–9,000; top positions, $9,000–12,000.

HISTORY MUSEUMS

Curator   Some directors recruit college-educated people with an interest in history, no matter what their educational backgrounds, and train them. If one is planning a long-term career in the field, it is far better to have as much formal training as possible. To be a curator at the Museum of History and Technology in Washington, D.C., one needs a Ph.D. At other history museums at least a master's degree is preferred, although a bachelor's degree often is acceptable. Ordinarily a student will major in American history as an undergraduate, then take graduate work in social, cultural, or industrial history, in the history of a region, or in the history of decorative arts. Training in museum techniques also is recommended since curators often have responsibility for restoring the objects in their care.

UNDERGRADUATE PROGRAMS

Heritage Foundation Summer
Fellowships (early American
history and fine arts), Deerfield, Massachusetts

Smithsonian research appointments (one-year appointments in civil, military, or cultural history, or history of science and technology), Smithsonian Institution, Division of Education and Training, Washington, D.C.

Western Michigan University History Department, Kalamazoo

Oregon Historical Society, with Portland State College, Portland

Summer Institute of American Maritime History, University of Connecticut, Storrs

Hagley Museum, with University of Delaware History Department (industrial history and museum techniques)

University of Delaware with Winterthur Museum (see listing under Art Museums: Curators)

National Academy of Sciences with National Research Council (graduate and postdoctoral fellowships in history of science or political science), Washington, D.C.

University of Michigan Museum of Art, with Henry Ford Museum

State University College at Oneonta with New York State Historical Association (history museum administration), Cooperstown

College of William and Mary Department of History (program in historical administration), Williamsburg, Virginia

National Trust for Historic Preservation (seminars in historical administration), Washington, D.C.

Salaries

Beginner, $6,000; experienced curator, $7,000–10,000; top positions, $10,000–15,000.

Archaeologist One ordinarily specializes in history as an undergraduate, or in art, then includes archaeological techniques and field experience in his graduate work.

University of Pennsylvania Museum, Philadelphia

University of Michigan Museum of Art, Ann Arbor

University of Missouri Department of Art History and Archaeology, Columbia

Princeton University Department of Art and Archaeology, Princeton, New Jersey

Archaeological Institute of America, New York, New York

South Dakota State Historical Museum, Pierre

University of Washington and Yakima–Fort Simcoe Project (archaeological research)

Logan Museum of Anthropology, Beloit, Wisconsin

Salaries

See History Museum Curator; for art museum archeology, see Art Museum Curator.

Educator   Undergraduate training in history and education frequently is required. On-the-job training also may be provided.

Salaries

Beginner, $5,000–6,000; experienced educator, $6,000–8,000; top positions, $8,000–10,000.

Registrar   A bachelor's degree in history is desirable, as is a background in business procedures and record-keeping. Technical training is acquired on the job. For techniques involved, see *Museum Registration Methods,* Dudley and Bezold.

Salaries

Beginner, $5,000–6,000; experienced registrar, $6,000–8,000; top positions, $8,000–10,000.

SCIENCE MUSEUMS

Curator   The major fields involved are anthropology, astronomy, botany, ecology, geology and mineralogy, oceanography, paleontology, and zoology with its many subdivisions.

In the largest museums, to become a member of the curatorial staff, one needs a Ph.D. or substantial work toward such a degree. In the smaller science museums, where the curator is somewhat less of a specialist, a Ph.D. would be welcome but a master's degree would be sufficient to obtain a position.

UNDERGRADUATE

Idaho State University Museum (summer course), Pocatello

Indiana University Museum, Bloomington

State University of South Dakota, Vermillion

Logan Museum of Anthropology, Beloit, Wisconsin

UNDERGRADUATE AND GRADUATE PROGRAMS

Museum of Northern Arizona (summer assistantships), Flagstaff

University of Colorado Museum, Boulder

University of California Museum of Anthropology, Berkeley

State University of Iowa Museum of Natural History, Iowa City

Smithsonian research appointments in anthropology, biology, astrophysics, and space science (see History Museum Curator Training)

GRADUATE PROGRAMS

National Academy of Sciences–National Research Council fellowships in biological sciences (see History Museums: Curators, Graduate Training)

Newark Museum, Newark, New Jersey

University of Michigan Museum of Art (museum methods in anthropology), Ann Arbor

Milwaukee Public Museum with University of Milwaukee, Department of Anthropology, Milwaukee, Wisconsin

Salaries

Beginner, $6,000–7,000; experienced curator, $8,000–13,000; top positions, $14,000–20,000.

Educator In the research museums, educators function as they do in all traditional museums, working with visiting classes and other groups. They usually have a bachelor's or a master's degree in one scientific field, plus some training and/or experience in education. In the science and industry museums, educators may have the added responsibility of conducting science demonstrations to illustrate various scientific principles. The qualifications generally are the same as for jobs in the research museums.

TRAINING PROGRAM

Museum of Science (two-year internships in museum science teaching) , Boston.

Salaries
Beginner, $5,000–6,000; experienced educator, $6,000–8,000; top positions, $8,000–15,000.

Exhibit Specialist A number of different jobs are involved, most of which are found only in the larger museums. *Exhibit Designers:* These men and women have responsibility for designing galleries and individual exhibits. Ordinarily they are products of art schools, but also may have experience in commerical, industrial, or advertising design. *Preparators:* These persons make models, assemble habitat groups and other dioramas, and create accessories—man-made grass, flowers, leaves, and other such items. Their training is obtained in art school and through an apprenticeship in a museum exhibits department. *Background Painters; Scientific Illustrators:* The first group paint the backgrounds one sees in dioramas; the second prepare detailed scientific drawings of specimens for displays and as illustrations in research reports. Both need art school training. *Taxidermists:* These are the specialists who prepare mammals, birds, and marine life for display. By and large, they learn their craft as apprentices in museums or commercial studios. Of all exhibit specialists, taxidermists are in shortest supply. Many museums which would hire one must turn to commercial firms or to taxidermists from other museums who freelance after hours.

Salaries
Exhibit designer: Beginner, $4,000–5,000; experienced designer, $5,000–10,000; top positions, $10,000–15,000.

Preparators, Background Painters, Scientific Illustrators: Beginner, $4,000–5,000; experienced craftsman, $5,000–10,000.

Taxidermists: Beginner, $4,000–5,000; experienced craftsman, $5,000–12,000.

Index